NEW BUDDHA WAY

This is the first book in a series of three called *New Buddha Way* setting out the life-changing way of the Buddha wholly in the context of contemporary and everyday life, relationships and work.

GEOFFREY HUNT founded New Buddha Way in Guildford, UK in 2002. He is Buddhist Associate Chaplain at the University of Surrey, and Professor of Philosophy at St Mary's University College (A College of the University of Surrey), Twickenham, London. He was Professor of Ethics at the University of Surrey, Guildford, UK until 2008. He has worked in Lesotho, Nigeria and Japan.

NEW BUDDHA WAY
Ethical Living

(Book 1)

Geoffrey Hunt

«LP» LALESTON PRESS Ltd

Laleston Press Ltd
PO Box 125
West Molesey
Surrey
KT8 1YE
United Kingdom

ISBN 978-0-9560673-0-2

Contact and information:

www.lalestonpress.com
info@lalestonpress.com

Printed and bound in Great Britain by Biddles Ltd,
King's Lynn, Norfolk.

CONTENTS

ACKNOWLEDGMENTS

I wish to thank my sister, Linda Hunt, for her leadership in nurturing NBW and her comments on an earlier draft of this book. My wife Beverley, who is a minister of the Anglican Church, is always helpful in exploring insights and we hold in our hearts both the Buddha and Jesus. I also warmly acknowledge the helpfulness and generosity of all those participants in NBW activities who have contributed ideas, energy and love.

Laleston Press is grateful to Wisdom Publications for kind permission to reproduce five excerpts from the Samyutta Nikaya (SN) and the Majjhima Nikaya (MN) in its 'Teachings of the Buddha' series as follows:

HOW TO USE THIS MANUAL

'New Buddha Way' is a *work* Manual, a lay instruction handbook to be used for *doing* things differently. It is in three separate but unified books which together intend to encapsulate the practices necessary for cultivating a new way of life.

Book 1: Ethical living. This is about the ethical living dimension of the Buddha's teaching, which in classical terms comprises right speech, right action, and right livelihood. This book also contains right effort, since it shows how an inner ethical endeavour phases into meditational practices. Note throughout that 'right' in this context means conducive (helpful) to enlightenment.

Book 2: Letting go. This is about meditation, which in classical terms comprises right effort, right mindfulness and right concentration. This book presents the second two.

Book 3: Letting in. This is about a general reorientation in understanding, in the wisdom and compassion of spiritual understanding, which in classical terms comprises right view (right understanding) and right intention.

The cultivation of this way of life requires the effort to follow all three dimensions. In the West there is a widespread misconception that 'meditation' (or just 'mindfulness') can work alone as yet another useful technique for our already weighty and untidy toolbox of therapeutic remedies. Whatever meditation can or cannot do alone, it cannot change your life in the way that enlightenment (spiritual understanding) can. For that all three dimensions are indispensable.

To forestall another possible misunderstanding in certain quarters I should perhaps say that this Manual, and indeed the very conception of a New Buddha Way, is intended as an introduction for ordinary people to an alternative way of life, and thus is also intended for contemporary society at large. In no way does it imply that individuals would not benefit more from a dedicated (probably monastic) teacher in *samadhi* and/or *vipassana* in a whole-of-life context.

The best way to use this Manual is in these stages:

1) One at a time, in the order published (Books 1, 2, 3), is the most productive way to read the three books.

2) Read the whole of Book 1, and then put it away for a few days. Do not move on to the next book until you have done the exercises in Book 1 several times.

3) Read Book 1 again more slowly and deliberately and spending time – repeatedly over a period - on each exercise.

4) After completing Book 1 and its exercises, it will be necessary to create a routine, and that is best done by joining a community of like-minded people. You could then return to the book whenever you feel you need some reminders or further guidance.

5) After several months have passed, follow the same procedure with Book 2, and later on for Book 3. As you go on, what will be really important is the regular practice within the Dharma community, as well as the integration into ordinary life of all three practices of ethical living, meditation and reorientation.

What the serious follower of this way will find is that while an earlier dimension prepares one for the next, the next one throws light on the previous, until the third dimension lights up the first and second, and so on. After all, there aren't really three dimensions, but just one way.

PREFACE

The New Buddha Way (NBW) network aims to bring the classical and life-changing teachings of the Buddha, and other spiritual teachers, into contemporary society, in a contemporary style, in ordinary English for 'ordinary' people.

The term 'New Buddha Way' is really being used in two ways in this Manual. It is an actually existing network in Surrey, UK which is a 'work in progress', adapting to circumstances and the needs and ideas of participants. It is also more than that, in so far as it is an ideal or aspiration for a new movement, which cannot be clearly defined at the outset but only outlined.

It is hoped that this Manual is one provisional element in a fruitful collective attempt to re-create a Buddha Way for our times and contemporary condition. A 'New Buddha Way' is a conception of a movement which brings the Buddha's teachings to fresh life in the age of science, technology, consumerism, globalisation and acute crisis that we now live in. Its heart, however, is not and never can be 'new' in the ordinary sense, but is eternal.

It has a long way to go, will have to confront many difficult issues and depend on much good will and competent teachers.

For a number of years NBW has been holding classes in the Buddha's practices of meditation, ethics and deep understanding in towns in Surrey, England. Groups of up to about two dozen people from all walks of life have been attending each class. These gatherings have provided basic orientation for NBW's regular (weekly) sessions of practice.

This small book is a response to a request for a short and simple book that provides an outline to these practices in plain English and at the same time suggests the criteria that a New Buddha Way might have to meet.

Everyone can be more peaceful and enlightened, even in this endarkening age – it is just a matter of regular personal practice and community support.

CHAPTER 1
CLINGING AND CRAVING

DIFFERENT STORY, SAME STORY

Pat spends quite a lot of time worrying. Work is difficult, the job is not always done well, people don't always get on with each other and often blame each other. Pat has sometimes been blamed, and feels quite stressed. Getting to sleep is not always easy, but a couple of glasses of wine often do the trick. Meanwhile, there are also family problems, and as soon as one is resolved, up pops another. Pat has happy moments, but often feels undervalued, misunderstood, and just plain worn out. Beyond work and family the world is quite a scary place. Pat does not always watch the news, but when it arrives in the living room there are scenes of bloody explosions, floods and hurricanes, petty political quarrels, dire warnings and fearsome forebodings. Pat has some concerns about health, and some wrinkles and hair loss are a reminder that old age and even death cannot be that far away. Pat thinks: 'If only I earned more then I could get a bigger pension, and feel a bit more secure in my final years'.

Meanwhile, in a not-so-wealthy part of the world thousands of kilometres away, Jose is having a problem finding work, and has to manage with casual labour here and there. Work is difficult, the job is not always done well, people don't always get on and they often blame each other. Jose has been on the receiving end sometimes, and feels quite stressed. Getting to sleep is not always easy, but a few glasses of a local brew often do the trick. Meanwhile, there are also family problems, and as soon as one is resolved, up pops another. Jose often feels undervalued, misunderstood, and just plain worn out. Beyond work and family the world is quite a scary place. Jose does not always watch the news, but when it arrives in the living room there are scenes of bloody explosions, floods and hurricanes, petty political quarrels, dire warnings and fearsome forebodings. Jose has some concerns about health, and some wrinkles and hair loss are a reminder that old age and even death cannot be that far away. Jose thinks: 'If only I earned more then I could save some money for my old age'.

Different story, same story. Different human being, same human being. Different human being, different remedies. Same human being, same remedy. Is there a remedy for our enduring dissatisfaction with a life that is more or less the same for everyone, man or woman, rich or poor, famous or not, clever or not, liked or not, of any race, nation or religion? 'Remedy' is not perhaps the right word. 'Palliative' perhaps. Is there some 'way of looking' at our common human character that is helpful in allaying or tempering what is harmful and elevating what is helpful to the peace of each, and the peace of all, as we live together for a short time on this tiny blue and green planet? The teachings of the Buddha, and other spiritually related teachers, suggest that there is such a way. It cannot eliminate the usual problems of life, and it cannot turn us into what we are not, but it can beneficially change our attitude to 'what we are'.

Parable: The Half-Glass

We all know this simple metaphor. Let us give our imagination free rein for a moment. Very thirsty, I come across a glass. If the glass contains half water and half air there may not be much I can do about it. That's what it is: half water, half air. However, it makes a great deal of difference to my satisfaction with the situation whether I consider it to be 'half empty' or 'half full'. If I feel I am in need of a drink of water, there are two ways I can look at the glass:

- The Usual Way (perhaps) is: "Oh No! Why is there only half a glass, I want more than that!"
- The Unusual Way (perhaps) is: "Oh, I am so grateful I have half a glass, let me drink and enjoy it!"

In both cases I drink the half-glass, and in both cases that's all there is. But in the first way, I begin with a strong desire for water, I gulp down the water, it doesn't last long enough, it's gone, I feel resentment arising, I crave more water, I feel dissatisfied about the water that is *not* there, and my frustration and dissatisfaction deepen. I feel an emptiness that cries out to be filled. Is there someone I can blame for this miserable situation?

In the Unusual Way I thank my lucky stars I have somehow come across some water, and what is more, it's in a glass! I savour every drop of the water as it touches my lips and trickles down my throat. I dimly sense some joy that this water is made for me and I am made for this water. I am water, and water is me. I note what a dependent thing I am - no water, no me. At the same, if this thirst-slaking experience did not exist, no person to savour water, what would 'water' be? What could it be? I feel gratitude and maybe a sense of connectedness. I might feel a fullness that invites me to empty myself of all craving. Blame is nowhere on my horizon. Instead I'd like to thank someone or something.

So here are two people and half a glass of water. They live in the same world. Or do they? Actually, their worlds are also quite different. One planet reached by means of two ways turns out to be two planets in the same place. Which one would you like to live on? The choice is yours.

16

CRAVING

'Craving' may not be a word we are very familiar with. Perhaps we can't really identify with it. Isn't that what 'addicts' feel? Yes, it is what addicts feel, in a self-destructively intense manner about *one* thing: alcohol, cocaine, heroine, tobacco and the like. But this is only a special case of addiction. In a broad sense we are all addicts, feeling a deep lack that we seek to fill with material gain, clothes and possessions; with pleasure, sex and entertainment; and with fame, recognition and popularity. While there is nothing 'wrong' with any of these any more than there is anything wrong with alcohol or cocaine in certain contexts (where they may be medicinal or have other benefits), there is something harmful in giving them an all-consuming prominence in one's life.

Putting aside the extreme case of substance addiction, there must be in all things a middle way between destructive indulgence and destructive self-denial. Usually a balance can be achieved with some awareness and effort. One needs to learn where the tippping point is. Applying this middle way to all things in life is known as 'wisdom'. Attaining wisdom is a slow and painful process, and is part of learning that the Unusual Way is ultimately the better way, in fact, the truly human way.

It should be possible to look into our cravings, our wants and see their nature. If we can do that it should be possible to lessen or soften them. But for that to be possible there would have to be a definite way of doing so, a way we can understand and apply. In the classical teachings of the Buddha we find this theme referred to as the Four Noble Truths: dissatisfaction, the cause of dissatisfaction in craving, the reduction and transcending of craving, and how to do the reducing and transcending. This means gradually moving from ignorance of the source of one's deep dissatisfaction, to freedom from ignorance and the peace that goes with that freedom.

If you have followed me so far, hopefully putting any minor 'if' and 'but' to one side for a while, the next questions will surely be: 'What actually *is* this Unusual Way?', and '*How* do I follow it?' Well, I'm, afraid you'll just have to read the rest of the book!

But before I describe this Unusual Way it is important to say something about how this is a way for you now in your 21st century life. It is not only a way for monks and nuns, not only for people in distant lands, not only for an elite of cushion-sitting intellectuals, and not only for people who have customs that are strange to some of us. It is for the man who drives a bus, the woman who manages an office, the man who delivers parcels, the woman who practises as a lawyer, the man who is a social worker, the woman who runs a flower-shop, the man who heads a Human Resources department, the woman who has just started her own business; in short, all of us as we are now.

If we know something about 'Buddhism' already (maybe by reading some books or attending a goup session) we might have some reservations. So, next I shall explain how the Unusual Way is thoroughly modern or contemporary. (If you are unbearably impatient to hear of the practices, then jump to Chapter 3, and return to Chapter 2 later.)

CHAPTER 2
A NEW BUDDHA WAY?

BUDDHA WITHOUT BUDDHISM

It is still early days in the growth of the Buddha's practices in the Western world. The West has misunderstood a great deal about the Buddha's practices. It seems many people already know what 'Buddhism' is without ever having really looked at it, let alone tried to practise it. We still hear things said like 'Buddhists are atheists', 'Buddhism is a middle-class philosophy', 'Buddhists believe in strange things like rebirth', 'Meditation is about stopping your thinking', 'Buddhism is just another fad', 'Buddhism is a pessimistic outlook', 'It undermines any ambition or dream you may have', 'Buddhists believe that ultimately there is nothing', 'Buddhism is a self-indulgent self-centredness', 'Buddhism is a withdrawal from the world'. All of these are false.

To begin with, 'Buddhism' as an 'ism' is a Western invention, an attempt to squeeze a group of practices and an understanding of (and attitude to) life into a belief system, ideology, philosophy or psychology. Closer to its origins people speak instead of 'Buddha sāsana', or literally, 'the teaching of the awakened one'. So, this Manual is not inviting or persuading anyone to 'become a Buddhist'. It is suggesting that if you feel an enduring deep-down sense of dissatisfaction with life then certain practices may help with that, bringing the kind of peace of mind that can only come with insight into the realities of life and what you are. This is obviously not about providing one with techniques for satisfying one's desires. Less obviously, it is not about *eliminating* the setbacks and calamities of life, but *reorienting* oneself to them, and even deploying them in aid of a deeper kind of peace and understanding.

Meanwhile, in the Eastern world those same practices have to a large extent, but not entirely, become rather fossilised in institutional and ritualistic forms, and have been given facile and literalistic interpretations. Sometimes these practices have degenerated and are merely paid lip-service to, and in some cases have disappeared. It will be many years, involving the efforts of many people, before the Buddha's liberating practices will be re-founded in the context and assumptions of the modern world, in which 'West' and 'East' no longer matter as far as those practices are concerned. It is quite possible that an understanding of those practices will throw new light on the teachings and lives of other great spiritual leaders.

So, could there be (or, is there already growing) a New Buddha Way, one which engages with the current and dominant manifestations of our assumptions about the human condition and the 'good life'? Many are beginning to perceive that these assumptions - consumerism, never-ending technological solutions, mastery over nature, individual freedoms without obligations or commitments - have led us into a dead end, and a dangerous one for the survival of human civilization (if 'civilization' it is).

The crisis that our world now faces on every front – cultural and philosophical, economic and environmental, political and social, moral and ethical – will no doubt have the effect of deepening religious fundamentalism, institutionalism and authoritarianism at the same time that it will push many people in the opposite direction and into a re-evaluation of the possibilities of open-hearted spiritual understanding.

The time is right for a fresh approach, one that maps the Buddha's way onto the *best* of the 'Western outlook'. Those of us brought up in the West do not have to try to be Tibetan or Japanese or Thai in order to adopt the Buddha's practices. Those of us in the East (India, Japan, China and other countries) do not have to reject the Buddha's practices simply because we reject so much of the painful past. Those practices do not in their essential message belong to the past, despite appearances. They transcend any culture and any historical period and can fit into the new as easily as they fitted into traditional cultures. In many ways those practices may *more* easily fit with some of the most liberating contours of 'Western civilization', while challenging those 'Western' contours that are leading the world to catastrophe.

What liberating contours? Those of openness and transparency, self-awareness, accountability and accessibility, equality and freedom of conscience, a spirit of negotiation and participation, and a questioning and critical attitude which seeks to get to the root of things.

THE PAWPER PRINCIPLES

The conditions for a new growth of the Buddha's teaching could perhaps be encapsulated in six guiding principles. I call them the PAWPER principles. The conception of a New Buddha Way is guided by these, and is open and receptive to its community of teachers and learners.

We now consider these more carefully one at a time. There a summary on Table 1.

Practice-based

NBW is not founded on beliefs (religious, philosophical, customary, historical, etc.), but on actual practices, and the inquiry and questioning that follows from such practices. These practices are inward as well as outward, and emphasize the former only to re-establish a human balance that can lead (I am jumping ahead to Book 3) to the enlightenment of no inner/outer.

By a 'belief' I mean (roughly speaking) a thought that something or other is questionably true, for example, that John is a good person or that Mars has no liquid water (which at present seems likely). It seems to me that recent decades have

Table 1 PAWPER

PRACTICE-BASED	Not belief-based
ACCESSIBLE	For every human being, and not just for an elite or a separate order.
WELL-FOUNDED	Built on the deepest core of existential understanding yet attained by human kind over milennia.
PARTICIPATORY	Involves everyone as equal in worth, while recognising diversity, and is wary of institutionalism.
ENGAGED	An affirmation, not a denial of life, and of the life we have now in the 21st century.
RADICAL	Lets go of the unworkable and literalistic assumptions of tradition, including those of 'Buddhist' tradition.

seen a quickening in the decline of religions from their spiritual insights and practices into an adherence to a set of 'naturalistic' beliefs and institutions. I say this not to reject religion, but to abandon what it has on the whole become. In the West many now wrongly think that attitudes and behaviour generally rest on beliefs, overlooking the fact that it is usually the other way around. A New Buddha Way does not ask anyone *to begin by believing* anything. This is not agnosticism or suspended belief, and it is not a matter of 'not believing anything'. It is simply a *different kind of approach* entirely. The new followers of the Buddha's teachings are not agnostics, not nihilists and not even sceptics, as we shall see in Book 3.

By a 'practice' in general I mean attitudes and behaviours. And, in speaking of the Buddha's 'practices', I am more narrowly speaking of the observation and potential redirection of my inner experience of thoughts and beliefs, sensations and feelings, attitudes and behaviours. It also includes the light this throws on other individuals and my relationship with others. For example, observing my experience of my own pleasures and pains, expectations and disappointments. Then, gradually moving on to much deeper aspects of my experience of being conscious, being human, being alive, 'being here' and even 'not being here'.

This shift from beliefs to practices is crucial in the age we now live in. Most importantly, if in trying to understand each other we begin with our beliefs we are certainly going to get into disagreements and arguments and this often leads to feelings of suspicion, hostility or even violence. If I want to find common ground I may try to persuade you that my belief is true or better. If you hear that I am a 'Buddhist', you may ask me 'What do Buddhists *believe*?'. Then, you listen and accept or reject. This is not a helpful approach. In fact, it is a hindrance. It is not a matter of being a 'Buddhist' or of believing this or that. Instead it is a matter of knowing how to look into yourself with some seriousness and determination to understand how you 'work', and uncover what you are in a deep sense.

What you may find there is your own distinctive mixture of the *same* human ingredients that make up every one of the fast-approaching seven billion humans on the planet. You can disagree with me about my beliefs (maybe, after all, there is some hidden liquid water on Mars!) but you cannot disagree with me about *my awareness of my experience*. There is another great matter that we cannot disagree about, approached in a certain way, but we shall have to wait until Book 3 for that. (Trying to fly before we can walk is not a good idea.) If I am aware that I am becoming angry, for example, then there is no room for disagreement, that is simply 'what is going on in me'. You might *believe* that a practice of developing the ability to be aware in such a way is a waste of time, of course. In that case, *your belief* might be getting in the way of responding to my invitation to try *doing* the same as I am.

You do not have to. That is what practitioners of the Buddha's way do in such circumstances. They don't try to *persuade* someone to adopt a belief; they *invite* them to join them in a practice. An invitation can always be turned down - no problem. Obviously, if you invite someone to dinner you are giving them an option, not imposing anything on them (usually). An invitation to dinner has little or nothing to do with beliefs. Imagine you invite someone to dinner and he asks, 'Do you believe in broccoli?' Or, 'Do you believe in dinner?'

Of course, 'believing *in*' is not the same as believing *that*'. They often get confused. 'I believe *in* my friends' means that I have some trust, or faith or confidence in them. In this sense too, you cannot begin the Buddha's practice if you do not have at least a glimmer of confidence that it *might* work for you.

Accessible

The New Buddha Way is an open invitation to anyone and everyone. You only need be human (or a sentient being) to qualify.

The New Buddha Way aspires to grow as a lay movement. That is, it is not specifically addressed to monks and nuns. It is not addressed specifically to intellectuals and people who can read dead languages (Sanskrit, Pāli, archaic Tibetan, etc.), although these languages are very interesting in many ways. If there's anything hidden that needs to be revealed then it is not to be found in a dead language but where you are hiding it in yourself.

There are some in the West who believe (or appear to believe) that the Buddha's teachings are only or principally to be found through some affiliation with and emulation of *the culture* of Tibet, Thailand, Burma, Vietnam, China, Japan or somewhere else in the 'East'. Well, they are invited to this practice too. The people of those countries or regions are also welcome. It might be refreshing to let go of 'Buddhism', that is, the Buddha's practice turned into a set of beliefs and institutions, and return to the practice itself in the context of our actual contemporary lives.

Of course, a New Buddha Way cannot be independent of culture as such, no more than any other human activity can be. For example, it is hopefully developing in England (among other places), and in the form of NBW. That's where the author of this book and his friends *happen* to live. NBW, is an 'experiment' in accessibility, that aspires to develop in English at the moment, and in ordinary English, although this language has no special privileges. It just *happens* to be rather common and useful at the present time, like Latin was at one time, or Chinese may be in the future.

NBW is not a *group* strictly speaking, since it has no boundary, inside/outside, and has no membership. Sometimes individuals turn up asking about 'joining', but one cannot join NBW in the club sense of 'join', because there is nothing to join. What you *can* do is follow the practices and take strength and lessons from others doing the same.

What is going on at an NBW session is an anchor for the practice and not a 'group' to be joined or a 'service' or ceremony to be a spectator at. Meditation and related practices are focussed in NBW sessions, but are meaningless if not taken into the ordinary life of each participant.

Anyone who has travelled the world knows that there are some broad differences in the assumptions, attitudes, relations and practices of peoples. The Buddha's practice of peace and insight may look strange and difficult to understand to people in one culture if it is all tied up in a completely different culture. It has always been tied up with *some* culture or another, and has always adapted and been adapted; it couldn't be otherwise. Now is the time for this practice to engage with the everyday culture of people in the streets of London, Paris, Frankfurt, Madrid, Rome, Stockholm, New York, Rio de Janeiro, Tokyo and elsewhere. And not only in the cities, but anywhere at all.

Well-founded

If we are going to follow some life-changing practice, we need some confidence that it is tried and tested, well-established and authentic. That is not enough, because it has to actually work for us, but it is a reasonable requirement. In the case of the Buddha's teachings we are fortunate to have a body of core teachings on how to practise (not on what to believe but on how to practise) that go back to his time. Since these teachings are about 2,500 years old it is not surprising that they have been interpreted, embellished and expanded by many of their followers. The result is a huge body of written works in many different languages, such as Indian languages, Tibetan, Chinese and Japanese. However, the Buddha had many followers over his 45 years of teaching in (what is now) India and Nepal and they appear to have done a good job of getting together to remember and recite what he said. After he died other followers wrote down the basics and, naturally, started introducing their own interpretations and embellishments. Over a period of time, as with all spiritual explorations, the indications of enlightening direction were given a literal meaning and officially ratified.

We are lucky that one collection of these earliest writings has survived almost intact and as a whole. It is the *Tipitaka* (meaning 'Three Baskets') which has been carefully maintained and protected by one line of his followers known as the *Theravada* (The Elders). This line is still to be found in Sri Lanka, Thailand and Burma, for example. Another ancient version exists in a Chinese line of followers. As one might expect, there have been all kinds of developments, commentaries and disagreements about this *Tipitaka* and its forebears, and in fact there are literalisms, inconsistencies, obscurities, lots of repetitions and a few absurdities in the *Tipitaka* itself. As the teachings spread from India northwards it changed its character into a more popular form known as Mahayana, the 'great vehicle' for all people. In Tibet, in particular, it absorbed all kinds of beliefs and practices that cannot be found in the Buddha's teachings.

All this does not matter that much for someone wishing to practise nowadays. You don't *have* to study anything, but you do need teachers. If anyone does choose to study the *Tipitaka* intensively, then after a while they would almost certainly see clearly what the coherent and consistent core of the teaching is. Literalistic interpretations would be the greatest snare, however. For the most part, the basis of the *Tipitaka* is neither a story about the Buddha nor about a nation or ethnic group and its trials and tribulations. It is about how *you do* the practices of peace and insight in order to ease the stress and suffering embedded in being alive, in living. That is the message of the *Tipitaka*.

So you are not asked to believe that the Buddha was anyone other than an exceptionally gifted spiritual teacher. His ordinary name was Siddhārtha Gautama (Siddhattha Gotama) and he was also known as Shakyamuni (meaning the wise man of the Shakya clan) and as 'the Buddha' (meaning 'the one who is fully awake'). He was not the only authentic spiritual teacher, before, at the time, or after. Many others were and are pointing in the same direction. (If, for example, one engages with the teachings *of* Jesus rather than the institutionalised story *about* Jesus, one will find many striking parallels.)

What the teachings make clear is that you too can be wise and fully awake. The burdens of deep dissatisfaction can be lifted. You can re-orientate yourself. But you do need to make a persistent effort – admittedly, not particularly easy in this busy consumerist age.

So a New Buddha Way would be based, as far as is possible, on a single, simple, coherent and consistent practice squeezed from the core teachings of the Buddha. This Manual of three books attempts to get these teachings across to anyone and everyone. It is not interested in arguing with scholars about origins and interpretations, for its ultimate test of validity is whether it goes some way to bringing the Buddha's fundamental teaching into everyday life now. We won't know unless we try it together.

The question of whether the Buddha's teachings are well-founded, then, is not really about the validity of an ancient compilation of books at all, but about what we find out about ourselves by ourselves. The books *might* help.

Participatory

We may summarise the teachings of the Buddha in one word: Dharma (or, Dhamma). This means several things: the *teachings* on insight into the ultimate truths of human life, and this *insight* itself, and these ultimate *truths* themselves. This is because to understand the teachings is not like grasping knowledge of arithmetic or plumbing or astronomy. The teachings really become teachings only when recognised and accepted into someone's life, and recognising them is itself to have insight, and the insight is a 'realisation' (reality finding itself in the individual, so to speak). So 'Dharma' stands for all three at once: the teaching, the accepting and the truth or reality.

This might seem peculiar at first, but it is very ordinary. We can more easily grasp it perhaps with a parable (below). The point I am coming to is that it is because the Dharma is this way that teaching and learning the Dharma *has to be participatory*, a shared practice of and between people. It is not a piece of knowledge held by one person (a kind of super-human) to be handed over to others who receive it passively.

Parable: The Taste of Broccoli

> Janet very much likes the taste of Broccoli. She tells her friend Fiona about it. Fiona has never tasted Broccoli, so how does Janet describe or explain it? Firstly, she tries to compare the taste of Broccoli to something else that Fiona is familiar with: cabbage and cauliflower. 'Broccoli is rather like Cauliflower, but stronger, a bit like cabbage and…' Fiona is now a little nearer to the taste of Broccoli, but what she has is the thought or image of Broccoli not the *taste* of Broccoli.
>
> Fiona persists with her questions about Broccoli. Later, Janet gets hold of some Broccoli, cooks it, invites Fiona over to dinner and serves it to her. Fiona tastes it; now she's got it. 'And how does it taste?' asks Janet. 'Well… I can't describe it, but it's good!'

Fiona has never tasted Broccoli, so how does Janet describe it? In fact, she cannot do so directly. She can do one of two things. One is to compare the taste of Broccoli to something else that Fiona is familiar with, like Cauliflower. In matters of spiritual or existential insight teachers might find themselves adopting that approach: 'What is the Kingdom of God like?' Jesus was asked. 'It is like a mustard seed,' he replied, 'and it grows and grows, into a tree, and even birds can lodge in it'.

The difficulty with this way of teaching is that the listener has to see through the analogy (or metaphor, symbol, parable, ritual) to what it 'stands for' or indicates. And they have to do so by themselves. But what it points at is precisely what they haven't seen before, so they might or might not be able to do that. It is a wonder that metaphors and parables ever work, but they often do, of course. (Art and poetry depend on them.)

So there is the danger of misunderstanding: the listener might take it literally. It depends on whether they are able to discern the difference as well as the similarity between metaphor and the 'thing indicated'. Literalism (connected with 'fundamentalism') causes a lot of difficulty and disagreement between us. People and groups have even killed each other because of it, sometimes on a large scale, and sometimes even within the same religion.

The second way is to *do* something: to go and get some Broccoli and invite Fiona to taste it. This requires effort on the part of the giver and the taker, the teacher and the learner. Very often we are not prepared to make any effort, partly because it takes us outside our 'comfort zone'. 'I'm happy with cabbage', says Fiona, 'Why should I try this foreign-sounding Broccoli-thing of yours?'

Now to come back to my point about the *Dharma*. How can it be the teaching, the learning and the thing taught at the same time? Well, think of the taste of Broccoli. The actually experienced taste (the reality) of the Broccoli is the only authentic teaching – the one that is bound to be effective under normal circumstances, even when all words fail. And where is this taste-experience? It is 'in' the learner; the person doing the tasting. At the precise point of tasting, it *is* the learner.

You may have noticed here that taste is a metaphor for insight, that which you attain through the Buddha's practice. As I said, the trouble with any metaphor is that either you get it or you don't. There are no guarantees. But the Buddha's practice offers many metaphors (and parables), many practices, many pointers and devices for attaining insight – most importantly, it is something one works one with and through other followers of the way. So there are infinite opportunities for 'getting it', sooner or later.

So now I can come back to my second point. Why is the Dharma necessarily participatory (a relationship between people), rather than a handing-over of a piece of knowledge? To return to the parable: this whole Broccoli-rigmarole was something going on between Janet and Fiona. Janet could talk as much as she liked *about* Broccoli – she might even fill a multi-volume book about it, *The World Encyclopedia of Broccoli* – but still the taste of Broccoli would be the real issue and talking or writing about that doesn't help, or doesn't help decisively. What would we make of someone who set themselves up as a leading Broccoli consultant and expert witness, but had never tasted Broccoli? Janet's analogies with cauliflower and cabbage might help to point Fiona in the right direction, but in the end they had to sit down to dinner together. Eating the Broccoli together, Janet winked, a big smile came over their faces: the mutual joy of Broccoli! No words were necessary.

To be honest, as far as Broccoli is concerned one can take it or leave it. No mutual joy is certain in this case. (It's a remarkable fact, but people have been known to dislike Broccoli.) But when it comes to the Dharma, it's another matter. To taste the Dharma is at once no longer to be oneself, but to be any and every human being, and even every creature, every thing. I cannot accept humility by myself, but only in relation to others, and this applies to all of us.

Thus the Dharma is something we can only cultivate together. When we divide ourselves up into factions, hierarchies and authorities we lose it. You might say it is the mutual understanding and striving of the human race. You already have what you need to enlighten yourself - you just forgot where you put it because together we have hidden it. Finding it – that's necessarily a community effort.

Participation is organic and free, and if flowing in the same general direction, it is immensely creative. It does not mean that anything goes, for there needs be a flow to it, not mere turbulence. Unfortunately, this flow once it emerges, may gradually crystallise, like a huge glacier grinding down everything in its path. This happens in the form of some authority-based religious institutions.

Then, some melting pools and subterranean springs can be very refreshing.

Engaged

Since it is necessarily an effort of human community, there can be no question of withdrawing from ordinary human life. The lessons to be learned are embedded in the human life that we have here and now. Undeniably, it can be a liberating step to withdraw oneself from the business of ordinary life completely for a period. The Buddha did so, Moses did so, Jesus did so, the Prophet Mohammed *pbh* did so. Countless others have found some degree of enlightenment by doing so, and continue to do so. Retreats are very beneficial, and there is no particular reason why every human being on the planet should not go on one at least once in their lifetime.

But retreats aside, we have to look honestly at ourselves, as we actually live from day to day, and do so together. Not as we have lived in the past, not as we wish to live in the future, but as we are actually living at this moment. The truth about ourselves does not primarily lie in history books, sociology treatises, psychology manuals and TV documentaries about the workings of the brain. It lies in what you said or didn't say to your partner or next door neighbour this morning, what you chose for breakfast, what you thought and felt in the minutes and hours of today, what you do for a living, what you bought or didn't buy, what made you laugh, your wants, irritation, fantasies, pleasant surpises, fears, worries, tiredness and doubts.

All the things that people think, believe, feel, and do day by day all around the world add up to the world we live in. *That's what the world is made of.* We may be mystified by what scientists tell us about tiny negative particles of matter, but we still have little understanding of the gross negative reactions and attitudes we humans have, or even what they are. Scientists may mystify us with their latest talk of 'dark energy', but the dark energy of our ignorance is already destroying us. Negative reactions and dark attitudes have killed and distressed many more of our fellows than negative nuclear particles. Our concern should first be ethical, and then technological. The Buddha, and other spiritual teachers, have always understood this. But somewhere in the blinding glare of technological progress and mass consumption a dark shadow has fallen over our ethical nature, over our deeper need to live in peace and understanding with each other. A menacing cloud of cleverness obscures the light of wisdom.

When we follow the Buddha's teachings by trying *to do* what he suggests, we shall almost certainly find that our attitude to all kinds of things around us will gradually change. This is not primarily because our 'beliefs' have been changed, but because we have come to see things in a new way. Our relatives and friends, our food, our homes, what we do for a living, our outlook on questions of environment, economics and politics all begin to take on a different meaning. *How* exactly, once again, is not easy to say. We are back to the taste of Broccoli. If we try to express it in words it would be something like this: we feel more peaceful, gentle, understanding, accepting and braver about everything going on around us, and this is because we are coming to see ourselves differently. And this is a different kind of 'difference'.

If my self-centredness is being dissolved then it follows that I want less, I reject less, and feel more at peace. Furthermore, if my self-centredness is weakened then I am more receptive and sensitive to what is going on around me. Since I am not the only important thing around, I notice the uniqueness and value in other things I might not have noticed before, and I am more inquisitive, respectful and accepting. In a curious way, while everything is seen to be unique, at the same time everything is connected too. The uniqueness is woven and interwoven into ever-shifting patterns.

I might now ask myself why I had never noticed all this before. The answer is because I was filled up with *my* thoughts, *my* feelings, *my* sensations, *my* body: I, me, mine. Where I was once preoccupied with myself, I am now becoming open to everyone and everything. I am, with others, engaging with the world in ways I could not have imagined. I may have thought I was engaged with it before – but that was to a large extent my *clinging* to what I wanted or did not want from the world, my craving for more of something (pleasurable, etc.) or less of something (painful, etc.).

Dharma parctice, then, is certainly about withdrawing from self-centred engagement with the world, to re-engage with the world selflessly (or less selfishly). The Buddha's practice is not just about sitting on a cushion meditating, but about our human life together. In the practice we are *dis*engaging from war on ourselves and nature, and engaging with what is necessary for peace, wisdom and sustainability.

Life cannot be affirmed from where we are right now, but only re-affirmed once we have re-oriented ourselves. With a global spiritual reorientation we would be in a well-founded position to provide clean water for all, food for all, education for all, care for all, artistic creativity and celebration for all. We have the material means to do these things now, but we don't because ethically and spiritually we don't know how.

Radical

When we face crises on all fronts it is a sure sign that our old ways of thinking have become dislocated from the realities of our lives. Nothing seems to make sense, and no obvious way forward can be envisioned. We may fall back into denial, cynicism or, much worse, become fearful and angry and seek someone to blame. In this situation it is vital to examine and challenge our way of thinking at its roots, that is, in a radical way.

An individualistic, pleasure-seeking and consumerist ideology has now spread across the world, setting fires in every corner, from California to China, from the Arctic to Amazonia. And we are ill-equipped; none of the viewpoints we have depended on for so long now seem to help us. There is surely something very inadequate in our broad views on the most important things: our moral and ethical values, the role of science and technology, our religions, our families and friendships, our way of life. Many of us know that something is very wrong, and feel disoriented, but have no clear idea of how to make any headway. There is a strong temptation to fall back on what helped us in the past, without thinking that this may make things worse, not better.

Maybe what we have to do is go back to square one. Put everything aside and start again. Is it possible to do this? Is it possible *not* to do this, if a climate catastrophe tears up the book of human history? Where would one begin? Would it be a matter of finding a completely new beginning in understanding our 'human nature'? Or, would it rather be a matter of refinding beginnings that had already been made and partially accumulated in human history and then misunderstood or lost? Have we really understood those who delved deeply into human nature, tried to tell us what we are and how to rise above it, and warned us of the consequences of remaining in ignorance?

All the great spiritual teachers over the millennia have told us, in one way or another, in different languages and with different imagery, that we are strongly inclined to be self-centred, blinkered, clinging and craving creatures, and that (as useful to short-term 'biological survival' as it may have been) this inclination is ultimately self-destructive and does not do justice to our potential. They have told us at the same time that there is a way to mellow and soften this inclination. The strange thing is that while on the whole the human race has accepted that this is true it has done one of two things. It has shrugged its shoulders and gone on as before, or it has gradually turned the recognition of this truth into yet another form of self-centred clinging (institutional religion, for the most part, as we know it today).

Perhaps our best hope is in a return to the core truth of these teachers in a radical spirit. By that, I mean making our best effort to understand the core truths, while cutting away from our minds all the subsequent encrustations of excuses, compromises, embellishments, misunderstandings and inconsistencies. It might be liking cutting back a tired and tangled garden, only to find that the following Spring pure white Snowdrops appear that one did not even know were there all along.

CHAPTER 3
WHAT I SAY

THE TASTE OF SALT

The teachings of the Buddha form a single coherent approach to life in which everything has its place. But this is not because it is a system of beliefs which is to be imposed on people and the world. Quite the opposite. It is because it teaches us to let go of imposition and let life speak for itself. But we have to listen very carefully and persistently. The Buddha sometimes said that the liberating teaching is unified in the way that the ocean has but one taste, the taste of salt. In the case of the Dharma the one taste is that of tenderising our judgments and freeing ourselves from human dissatisfaction. This dissatisfaction takes many forms on different levels.

On quite an obvious level we all suffer pain, frustration, illness, grief, loss and disappointment. But it will certainly not escape our notice that we may, especially if we are 'lucky' and 'talented', enjoy pleasures, success, good health, wealth, and long life. The nice experiences might just outweigh the nasty experiences in the lottery of life. Maybe most of us think this way. It is to think of a life as a kind of cosmic casino, with candy and sex as a reward, and cancer and divorce as a penalty. If we get the former we are happy, and if we get the latter we are sad.

This is one way of looking at dissatisfaction. As something that comes and goes. But are we looking at ourselves hard enough? And with fairness? Is there an underlying and abiding dissatisfaction? Take death. That's a bit awkward, isn't it? We can't wager, play games or negotiate with that. Maybe that's like being thrown out of the casino. Not for a month or year, but for ever.

One way of dealing with that is not to think about it at all. If I do contemplate my own death, thereby making myself uncomfortable, I have (eventually) to put up with another fact: I am not the only one who is going to die. Everyone I love is going to die, and some of them before I do. Furthermore, I almost certainly don't know *when* they will die or when I will die.

As if that isn't enough, it might occur to me that *everyone* that is alive right now (2008) – about 6,700,000,000 people like me – will be dead in just 125 years (assuming there is not a global annihilation before then). Most will be dead within 80 years. Billions of other people will have been born, of course. But they will die too. It's all a bit scary; far better not to think about such things! (Are you now thinking of putting this book down, and picking it up again 'later'?)

Most of us will accept, perhaps reluctantly, that it is far better to accept whatever has the unfortunate qualities of being both thoroughly unpleasant and inevitable. For example, what a difference it might make to me to grasp fully how precious every single moment of my life is! But I am jumping ahead. First we have to clamber over a rugged stone wall before we can enjoy the peaceful pasture on the other side. So, returning to the liberating ugliness of death for just another couple of unbearable paragraphs.

Before one dies there is the prospect of becoming unattractive, sick, or at least weak and fragile, and seeing loved ones in such a state. Before these things happen we also have to suffer the fear and anxiety of their happening or the uncertainty of whether they will happen and when. And speaking of fear and anxiety, it may occasionally dawn on us that everything else that is most dear to us, could be lost at any moment: homes, furniture, gardens, money, job, hair, teeth, eyesight, memory, photo albums … you name it.

During certain periods in our lives many of us, wherever we are, will pose some disturbing and unanswerable questions: What am I really? Why am I me rather than anyone else? Where do I come from and where am I going? Is there any point in life? Is time an illusion? Is there something all-powerful behind it all? The questions are hard to pose in any meaningful way, and there is not even a way of determining whether they *are* meaningful. Behind such questions may be feelings of unease, bewilderment, fear, emptiness and even desolation.

I am not making all this up just for a shock effect. If anything is shocking here it is that I am *talking* about it. We are thinking about a largely taboo area. You may already be concluding that this book is hardly likely to be a best seller!

The point has been made. The Buddha's starting point is that there is an abiding dissatisfaction or anxiety or fear in human life, and that if we do not face it and overcome or transcend it (or at least soften it) then it will push us into all kinds of disappointing, destructive and self-destructive fantasies. As we look at the incredible follies and man-made catastrophes of the last one hundred years, and those yet to come, we may begin to see that the Buddha was onto something big, perhaps too big for us to accept.

ETHICS

Many people think that the Buddha was only really interested in sitting under a tree meditating; meditation is what he was all about. This is not right, however. Everything he was about has the 'taste of salt', that is, all his teaching and his life are about liberation from abiding dissatisfaction. This liberation is about the *whole* of your life, and the whole of our lives together. We do not understand what we are, so we do not behave in accordance with what we are, so we do not practise a way that would help us to understand what we are, so we do not understand what we are, so… It's a vicious circle. The whole of human life is caught up in this fantasy-land vicious circle. It would be appealing to many if meditation were another quick fix, but it does not really work unless it is part of a wider re-orientation.

Our ignorance, our lack of compassion for ourselves and each other, and our unawareness and uncontrolled minds are all stitched together in one fabric. What binds this process of endarkenment (growing darkness) is my sense of self, which attaches, craves and clings. It takes hold, holds on tightly and craves for more. This is not about being 'selfish', for even those who are not 'selfish' in the usual judgemental sense will cling to the sense of self. This is not a 'bad' thing; but just how things are. The centrifugal force of this endarkenment is my sense of being a separate, independent 'self' that wants, wants to be more, wants to be secure, wants to live, wants more of everything. Thus our moving towards understanding, towards ethical living, towards awareness and measured minds are also of one piece. What unites that (inward) centripetal movement of enlightenment is the letting go of 'I', 'me', 'mine'.

My point now is that the Dharma is as much about ethics as it is about meditation, and as much about deep understanding (a spiritual sense) as it is about ethics. The sense of being 'myself', that needs to be protected and built up, manifests itself in my constantly attaching to the things that can apparently serve those two purposes: *clinging* to them when I 'have' them, and craving for them when I do not have them or do not have enough of them. At the same time I am constantly excluding or *rejecting* anything that apparently hinders or threatens or undermines those things that I am clinging to.

Pride is my clinging to my sense of 'I' and 'me' and all those things that 'make me' what I am in my own eyes: my name, my gender, class, race, achievements, role in society, loveable-ness and so on. Supporting this sense is all that I have or possess: 'my' and 'mine'. My body, my clothes, my home, my personal belongings, my partner, my family, my friends, my reputation, my money, my qualifications and so on. When the sense of 'I', 'me' 'mine' is threatened or apparently threatened there will be a reaction such as indignation, humiliation or anger. This sense is expressed in all that we say, do and relate to, in short, to all that we are.

MINDFUL SPEAKING & LISTENING

What more obvious place to start on the Unusual Way of enlightenment, on unravelling the Usual Way of endarkenment, than considering the ethics of the way we speak. We cannot really take speaking in isolation from the rest of our understanding, attitudes and activities, but we have to start somewhere in a clear and specific way. Speaking seems a simple enough matter – but is it?

We are speaking with each other (and even inwardly to ourselves) from morning to night, but generally pay little here-and-now attention to the assumptions and intentions underlying this speech. The Buddha taught about this, and he distinguished between skilful speech and unskilful speech. That is, between the ignorant speech that springs in one way or another from our clinging and our rejecting and the wise speech that springs from letting go of clinging and rejecting. His aim is not divisively to classify some speech as 'bad' or 'wrong' and other speech as 'good' or 'right'. His aim is to generate awareness and insight into ourselves. By 'ignorant' he does not mean 'stupid', but simply 'without knowledge', *unaware* of the cloying forces and habitual channels underlying our speaking and listening.

The Buddha suggests that we might begin to develop a liberating awareness of speaking by paying attention to five aspects, as in Table 2 below. We should not take this too rigidly, and it is not meant to be comprehensive, but just a point of departure and guide. We should also keep in mind that what he teaches us about speaking is not meant to be used as a means of divisively judging others, for that would be to turn his intention into its very opposite. I also emphasize that it is not meant as a standard of perfection, setting us up for failure, but is simply a guide to gradually developing one aspect of self-awareness and peace.

Table 2: Five Aspects of Speaking and Listening

	HELPFUL	UNHELPFUL
ATTITUDE	With good will	With ill will
INTENTION	Beneficial	Harmful
TRUTH	True	False
MANNER	Gentle	Harsh
TIMELINESS	Timely	Untimely

Attitude

Speaking is not always what it appears to be on the surface. It will reflect a person's beliefs, past experiences, needs, wants and defences. Speaking, or any part of it, may flow from a negative orientation such as cynicism, or from particular feelings such as resentment or anger, which may often be concealed. Such an attitude will be *revealed*, sooner or later, even if the speaker is not aware of it. The listener too may not be aware of it, or only dimly in feelings of uneasiness. The listener may even join in the negativity, and the whole dialogue becomes a feedback cry of unhappiness expressed as negative opinion. They may depart from each other none the wiser, and at worst have reinforced in each other a rejecting outlook, convinced it is 'realistic'.

A negative orientation of reactions is often revealed in speech that begins with 'People do or don't do X', where X is something negative. For example, 'People don't really care', 'People drive badly', 'People are chasing money'. There are three important things to note about this way of speaking. Firstly, nothing good is being said about 'people' (such as 'People are kind', 'People drive well', 'People are not chasing money'). Secondly, it is a generalisation. There may well be truth in saying '*Some* (or many) people don't care' just as there is some truth in saying '*Some* (or many) people do care', and so on. Even then, other questions could be asked about such statements (see Table 2). Thirdly, the speaker is curiously *absent*, even though they are speaking. That is, when the speaker says 'People don't care' are they including or excluding themselves? If they are including themselves then they are making a confession at the same time that they are tarring everyone with the same brush. If they are excluding themselves then they infer that they are the uniquely caring person on the planet.

Neither of these alternatives is very convincing, which leads us to conclude that statements like '*People* do or don't do X' are empty of information and are simply direct expressions of a negative outlook (like making a rude gesture), which is unhelpful both to the speaker and to the listener. The negative outlook will have its causes in the person's life and character, and the point is not to condemn or reject this but understand the underlying unhappiness. That is, not to condemn oneself for speaking in this way, nor not to condemn others for doing so, but to acknowledge, recognise, understand. With self-awareness may also come the question: 'Is this attitude me; is it mine?' With that question we are on the edge of insight and liberation.

Speaking, or any part of it, may also flow from a positive orientation such as helpfulness or equanimity, or from particular feelings such as gratitude, generosity or joy over someone's else's happiness. These too may be concealed, for example, where there is fear of seeming weak, naïve or sentimental.

An attitude or orientation is also behind our listening. I can always examine myself and ask: 'Am I listening with a negative attitude of irritability, a positive one of kindness or a neutral attitude?' The attitude will make a great deal of difference to what I hear, and being aware of my attitude will also make a difference. Naturally, speaking and listening feed off each other in a cycle of reactions. The attitude shaping what I say to you will affect the attitude shaping what you say to me which in turn will affect the attitude shaping what I say to you which… Awareness is a way of breaking out of this cycle of reactions.

Not speaking is always an option. What pressures us to speak, even when silence is the best option? The Unusual Way of not-speaking can sometimes say more than the Usual Way of speaking.

Intention

There is an intention behind everything we say or omit to say. An intention will often be a manifestation of a wider attitude. The intention may be obvious ('How do I get to the bus station?' implies that I have an intention of getting to that particular place), or it may be indirect or oblique. When it is the latter the intention may be kindly or exploratory, for example, or it may be indirectly comparative ('Is yours as good as mine?') or to 'size up' the listener ('Are you as great as I am?') or tacitly to get something from the listener ('Are you influential?', 'Can you do something for me?'). It may even be demeaning, or an expression of prejudice and rejection.

Speaking and listening rest on a network of tacit assumptions, of which the participants may not be aware. In speaking with enhanced awareness many of those assumptions will come to the surface and one may choose to speak more helpfully and less harmfully.

The important point is simply for me to develop some awareness, especially at critical moments, of what I am intending to bring about by what I am saying: is it helpful or unhelpful to others and to myself as a person seeking wisdom and peace?

The Buddha does not mean to make us neurotic about every conversation. We can not always be clear about what our intentions are in saying something. Furthermore, we may not be clear what someone else's intentions are when we are listening. But we can give them the benefit of the doubt.

Misunderstandings may arise, and our attitude and intentions will be crucial at those moments. What, then, does it mean to be 'generous' in interpreting what another person is saying? We all tend to 'infect' the words of others with our own intentions, preconceptions, expectations and desires.

When someone else's speech is unskilful, how do we 'deal with it' skilfully? Do we sometimes avoid responsibility for our attitudes and intentions in our speech, for example, shifting responsibility with: 'You *made* me angry!?

Truth

Truth would appear to be a simple matter. Either a statement is true or it is not. On the whole one should say what is true rather than what is false. However, a lot of what we say does not consist of 'pure' statements, but of questions, suggestions, expressions of emotion and preference, commands, explorations, thanks, hints and so on. And a lot depends on the context of the conversation and the setting. When we are making a statement it is not always as clear cut as 'It is raining', and even that is sometimes debatable. Is a light and fleeting drizzle really 'rain'? Am I *really* just making an excuse for not walking down to the shop for the loaf of bread that is needed?

Our attitudes and intentions will make a world of difference to the truth or falsity of what we are saying. If my attitude is one of ill-will then even a true statement may aim to hurt. If my attitude is one of conceit or arrogance then my true statement may aim to boost my ego rather than throw any light on the situation under discussion.

Even a true statement may mislead, if it is said in a context in which other significant matters are deliberately omitted. In other words, one can lie by telling a falsehood or more subtly lie by telling a truth. When there are strong interests or emotions behind what we are saying then it may be very hard to admit that one is not being truthful. In many ways the most harmful kind of lie is the one that one tells to *oneself.* This is closely connected with the 'ignorance' that the Buddha claimed lay behind so much of our human conflicts and unhappiness. For the Buddha 'ignorance' was not so much about not knowing the truth, but not 'wanting' to know the truth, that is, not admitting it. One might say that the entire teaching of the Buddha is this: the human race is deceiving itself about life, but there is also a human potential to stop doing that.

When we look into ourselves honestly, observe our reactions, and note the arising of envy, spite, impatience and resentment can we *acknowledge* their existence without passing destructive judgement on ourselves? When we note the arising of kindness, generosity, patience and gratitude can we acknowledge them without smugly patting ourselves on the head? Do we find it easier to be truthful about others than about ourselves? In fact, *can* we be truthful about others if we cannot be truthful about ourselves?

Manner

Imagine that you are at a meeting in which some matter has been hotly debated and you have not yet said anything. You suspect that a significant truth, the 'elephant in the room', has been avoided by everyone so far, maybe because it is difficult to raise without conflict breaking out and someone getting blamed. It seems to you that those present are afraid to mention it, and as a result the situation is becoming increasingly dishonest. 'I am going to speak up', you say to yourself, but how do you do it? It seems timely, you feel that you have good will towards everyone, your intention is to break the deadlock so that a good decision can be made, and you will clearly state the truth.

Unfortunately, you feel rather nervous, and when you speak you do so in a rather direct way, with a loud and emphatic voice, which is taken by some present to be a supercilious manner. Someone snaps, 'We know that! Do you think we're that stupid!'. You might be tempted to snap back. From then on nearly everyone's manner of speaking seems to rapidly deteriorate, with rudeness, interruptions and sarcasm. Perhaps everyone joins in the fray, some feel offended and before you know what the good decision you had hoped for is even further away than it was before. Endarkenment reigns. What has gone wrong here, and could it have been prevented?

The manner of speaking can also take the shape of cynicism, exaggeration, hurtful jokes, sneering, being triumphant, demeaning words, cursing, giving the wrong impression, flattering, patronising, manipulation and 'spin', speaking behind someone's back, and so on. It can also take the shape of the opposite of these – which is a choice one is free to make, but one needs to be *aware* that there is a choice.

The manner of speaking is always significant, but even more so in situations like this, in which an evaded truth needs to be brought into the open. This is a real test, and it is not easy to get it right. Since everything else is in place – attitude, intention, truth, timeliness – the ingredient that could have promoted enlightenment here is a gentle, humble and reassuring tone. Admittedly, this is hardly the dominant style these days, but one can understand why someone in the position of Kofi Annan (at one time, Secretary-General of the United Nations) found it essential. And have you noticed Nelson Mandela's *manner* of speaking? We can all take a leaf out of their books perhaps.

Gentleness of manner is not an optional extra, and not to be affected, but cultivated in the context of the whole Dharma it promotes. It comes with a subduing of the sense of I, me, mine which is the main source of all our human woes. It is not about mere politeness, which sometimes papers over an underlying ill-will, but something deeper, connected with letting go of clinging/rejecting words, and indeed letting go of talking too much.

The manner of listening is sometimes what directs a conversation. However, well-intentioned and gentle you may say something to a certain person it may touch a nerve and that person will feel hurt. They may respond by accusing you of being hurtful.

Even in 'Buddhist' circles I have sometimes heard a person use 'Right Speech' as a weapon of revenge: 'You are not using right speech in speaking to me!'. But the points being made here are for *self*-analysis, not as more weaponry to throw at other people.

Timeliness

Timeliness was mentioned in the example above. It is also crucial, and like the manner of speaking it can be the one missing ingredient which undermines everything else. Take the truth, for example. Is it a good thing to tell the truth just because it is the truth, regardless of whether this is or is not the best time to do so? To take a rather crass example, is it *always* right, no matter the circumstances, to give immediately to a person one cares about some news that will distress them? Should one not, in *some* circumstances, wait a while perhaps? There is also possibility of mentioning some matter too late (or not at all), perhaps because I did not care enough to remember it, or because it is not in my 'interest', or because I am afraid of the anxiety or embarrassment that might follow.

As in the example of the meeting (given in the previous section) it may be beneficial for individuals to work towards a truth themselves, rather than be told by you. Waiting to see what emerges may be enlightening for all in a way in which having it handed to one 'on a plate' would not be. However, a moment might come when it seems right and proper to say what needs to be said. That might require courage. In some circumstances the moment may pass, and saying it later would not be as beneficial. What often gets in the way of this discernment is the usual human baggage of personal attachments and rejections. If only I can drop the baggage the right moment will often appear of its own accord.

You can begin now. It is not enough to understand intellectually what I have said here – one has to start *doing* something with oneself. Here's an exercise.

Exercise: Mindful Dialogue

> Next time you are in a group of people (for example, at work or at a social or family gathering) who are speaking negatively of a colleague, for whatever reason, pay attention to what *you* are saying, what you are tempted to say and what you do not say. (Note, it is what *you* are saying that will help you, not what others are saying.) Observe, your mood, what it is you are saying, why you are saying it here and now, your intention or motivation in saying it, the manner in which you are saying it, and why you are saying it to *this* person or persons. Also observe how you are listening, and what you are bringing to your interpretations of what is being said.

There is more to communicating with awareness than speaking and listening. There are body language and facial movements, and tone, volume inflection, and there is writing and recording, phoning, emailing and blogging. There are choices about to whom I speak and when and why, and considerations of why I may speak differently to one person compared with another. Should the position or status of the person to whom I am speaking make a difference, and if so what kind of difference? We are now moving into the area of the ethics of action. Speech is, after all, a form of action in and upon the world. The Buddha has a great deal to teach us about action.

CHAPTER 4
WHAT I DO

CHOICE?

Why should I pay particular attention to what I do in my everyday relations with other individuals. I may already have some idea of 'who' I am (what sort of person I am), but the idea may not actually fit my demonstrations of who I am in my day-by-day, hour-by-hour behaviour. My actions show who and what I am. A lot that has been said about speaking can also be said about acting generally. But I shall avoid repeating myself, but try to throw some further light from different perspectives.

The teachings on personal action are, like all the Buddha's teachings, ultimately based on the fact of the abiding dissatisfaction that results from deep-seated craving, and the possibility of freeing oneself from such craving and thus from the dissatisfaction. Actually, our attaching, clinging, craving, as well as our rejections, appear most vividly in what we do as individuals, in our relationships with other individuals such as family, friends, acquaintances, strangers and those perceived as different from ourselves.

The Buddha's teaching suggests that most of what we do – and the when, where, how, and why of it - is a matter of ingrained attitude and reaction, not a matter of conscious choice. Each of us is formed by a long, patterned series of causes and conditions. Mostly, we do not really choose what sort of person we are. Modern scientific research bears this out. Although we can change, it is difficult and sometimes appears near-impossible. But the Buddha had enormous confidence in the capacity of human beings to liberate themselves from themselves, if they go about it in a certain way. After all, *he* liberated himself, but only with the aid of previous teachings;

and with his own independence of mind, courage and effort. Everyone has some degree of these virtues, with very few exceptions. We know this because we see them at work every day in the notable things that people achieve. The Buddha suggests that we tap into that energy and courage and at least channel some of it, some of the time, into nurturing the roots of wisdom and peace.

If we can put enormous and sustained effort into learning a musical instrument, or a sport or physical fitness, or learning a foreign language then how much more important it must be to channel effort into self-understanding and wisdom. Just consider how much time we spend standing before a mirror, attending to our faces and bodies, our hair and teeth, our clothes and shoes, and then compare it with how much time is spent on developing a wiser outlook on life, on seeing into the nature of one's short life time.

As we shall see, while the key thing for a 100m athlete may be their muscle tone, the key thing for a 'wisdom athlete' is self-awareness. If we have little awareness of ourselves then change in the direction of wisdom and peacefulness is almost impossible. Meditation provides us with certain exercise equipment for developing self-awareness (see Book 2). But, just as we have to start learning a sport or to play a musical instrument with some very basic movements and by addressing certain hindering habits, so in following the Buddha's Dharma we need to do the same.

Karma

When the Buddha teaches about what we do in everyday life, in his own language, he speaks about *karma* (*kamma*). It is just an ordinary word in his language, used in ordinary contexts. It means 'action', although it has now been widely misunderstood. Some have taken it literally, some have turned it into a belief, some into a hard-to-believe metaphysical system, something doctrinal, and something to argue about. Karma has in some quarters turned into an institution.

There is no doctrine of 'Karma' (capital K) that you have to believe in order to follow the Buddha's teaching, although you may have to believe it in order to join some 'Buddhist' groups.

The Buddha was not interested in philosophical theories or metaphysical beliefs. He said so many times himself, and also said that he had no secret teaching. As far as he was concerned what he had to teach could be discovered by people for themselves, if only they would look hard enough, sincerely enough and in the right way. So, I will not show off some mysterious doctrine of *karma* (and see 'rebirth' in Book 3) but simply speak of action and reaction, doing and not doing, acting and reacting, and the like.

However, one thing does need to be said about our individual action, which should be obvious, but which we have forgotten in our contemporary culture, and which the currently confused notion of 'karma' does dimly reflect. While it would be helpful to let go of any clinging to the metaphysical view of 'karma' as some kind of return after death, there is something vital we need to understand. That is, my every action on something or someone is *at once* an action on myself. If 'karma' has any meaning at all then it is that and only that; that is its spiritual meaning.

We can all see this if we wish, but usually pay no attention to it. There is a vivid saying in the Buddha's teachings that getting angry with a person is like picking up a burning coal with one's bare hand to throw at that person. When I am *directing* anger towards you I am *suffering* anger. I have made this feeling my own. If I had a choice would I take ownership of such a thing? I have taken hold of anger like I might take hold of a hot coal. Not very wise. The intended destruction, which may or may not result, is at once and necessarily a self-destruction. This is especially clear if my anger has no impact on you. I am left feeling the discomfort, even the pain, of the anger. I may feel foolish or regretful. I have attached to this arising feeling which is here and now endarkening my life. This is not a *consequence* of the anger, it *is* the anger. I repeat: It is the anger itself.

Every single action is in its very nature an inner 'boomerang'. You might say, in religious language, that the 'Day of Judgement' is built into every nook and cranny of our lives. Every action is its own light or darkness to the actor, and does not await consequences. In this spiritual sense, those who set out to hurt others never 'get away with it'.

We need to keep this in mind throughout the following consideration of action.

Do's and don'ts

If we understand the Buddha's teaching about craving, clinging and the way to subdue them on the path to a more enlightened life, then there will be little need for attachment to rules. In fact, a strong attachment to rules is quite likely to give rise to poor judgement, and an insensitivity to the actual situation. The Buddha's ethics is not based on rules. Putting aside a monastic context for the moment, we find that nearly all 'Buddhist schools' lay some emphasis on five abstentions. These are: to refrain from killing, from stealing, from lying, from sexual misconduct and from intoxicants. While for some people this is just common sense, others yield to the temptation to build a whole theory on these, and endless refined arguments may follow.

If one understands the heart of the Buddha's ethical teaching, which resides in letting go of clinging, then it will be obvious what these five supposed rules amount to, and *attaching* to them is not necessary or helpful.

Negligent and cruel destruction of life is generally based on clinging, craving and rejection, and is endarkening. There is no fixed rule here absolutely prohibiting the taking of life under *any* circumstances. An *attitude* of respect for life is what the Unusual Way points to.

The same goes for taking what does not belong to you, telling untruths, some sexual behaviour and some 'taking of substances'. These should be understood in the context of what helps or hinders the following of the Buddha's way, and all that one can say in general terms is that anything likely to be harmful or destructive to you and others will be a hindrance. But the judgement in any case has to be made *by you*, that's the point. Dogmatically following a rule cannot be enlightening. An absolute rule against even a single glass of wine at a family gathering is not in the spirit of the Buddha's teachings, although intoxication and alcoholism would clearly be hindrances needing some attention.

This is not a plea for subjective chaos, but rests on the attitude of letting go of self-centredness and dogmatic attachments that is so conducive to social peace and harmony. Laws and regulations certainly have their social function and importance, but even they have their exceptions, mitigating circumstances and interpretations.

Hopefully, this will all become clearer in what follows.

USUAL ACTION

The main aspects of our usual action are in Table 3. Again, we should not take this too rigidly, and it is not meant to be comprehensive, but just a point of departure and guide. We should also be able to relate this table to speaking and listening, as discussed in the previous section.

Table 3: Four Aspects of Usual Action

ORIENTATION	Giving	Taking
ATTITUDE	Hostile	Kind
INTENTION	Pleasure, praise, fame, gain	Pain, blame, ill-repute, loss
AUTHENTICITY	Sincere	Insincere

Orientation

It may help to think of any human being's behaviour as based on an orientation of reactions along an axis running from a negative pole of taking and defending to a positive pole of giving and trust. Negative pole and positive pole, as in a magnet, always go together. So this is not meant to condemn or to raise some people above others. Depending on circumstances, everyone gives and takes, everyone is defensive and trusting. That is just how things are with us. What is important for *me* is understanding where I am taking my place on this axis; not where other people stand, but where *I* stand.

Jumping to conclusions about this with an unexamined view of myself is not helpful. Nor is it helpful to excuse myself with 'I have to be suspicious and get what I can, because people are nasty', or pat myself on the head with 'I am a nice person, it's other people who have a problem'. What *does* help is catching myself in the act of reacting at either end of the axis. As I catch myself more and more I begin to distance myself a little, and see that there is some choice, and learn to choose the pole that makes the 'inner boomerang' ineffective. Understanding this, I can see that I do this not in order to praise or condemn oneself, but simply to be aware of how I really am in my potential to act or not act in particular ways with other people. My actions flow from my orientation.

A basic orientation of giving or taking is subject to 'ups and downs', but there will be a general trend in a person. This is their character. It is easier to see in another person whether, on the whole, they have a generous spirit (giving) and grateful one (taking), or a mean spirit (giving) and ungrateful one (taking). It is not so easy to see this in oneself perhaps, but this is what is important.

These poles are associated with clinging/rejecting and letting go, which is fundamental to the practice. If I am nearer to the clinging pole then that manifests in a higher level of grasping, wanting more, taking more, manoeuvring to take even more. While I cannot but 'take' into order to live (e.g. destroy and eat some other forms of life), there is a point at which it may tip into the very point I give to my life. Hence 'greed'. That is the direction of endarkenment.

When I take I seem to have gained – but every gain is a loss somewhere, every gain leaves a hole somewhere, and that hole waits for me and us in the darkness. I pull up a potato from the ground because I am hungry. The potato feeds the hunger, the pulling up leaves a hole. The potato has been transferred from the soil to my belly. The hole has been transferred from my belly to the soil. Now the soil is in want, and the creatures who depend on that lump of soil are in want.

It is worth noting that taking can sometimes be the outward form of giving, as one accepts graciously in some situations. And giving can be a form of taking, such as when it done with the intention to show off or cause guilt.

If I am at the letting-go pole then I am aware of a moment-by-moment balancing act: the distinction between what my (our) very physical existence demands and what my (our) humanity demands (wisdom, insight, compassion, peace). That awareness makes a tremendous difference to me and everyone. That is the direction of enlightenment.

A generous orientation appears in how far I lean towards putting at the disposal of other people, other creatures and the environment my time, effort, support, sustenance and so on. A grateful orientation appears in how far I lean towards a new readiness to give even more when I receive time, effort, support, sustenance from other people, creatures and the environment. It is a virtuous circle. Giving is taking, taking is giving. It's the positive form of the 'inner boomerang'. In this case I don't have to duck.

When the hole has been transferred from my belly to the soil, I understand that the soil needs care.

Attitude

The nature of action, as outlined above, clarifies the importance of my general attitude to others along an axis of hostility at one end and kindness at the other. At one end of the axis I may catch myself acting with anger, frustration, irritation, resentment, sneering, impatience and the like. (And I have already learned that if my ill-will aims to hinder you in some way, it is hindering me completely.)

At the other end I may catch myself acting with genuine kindness, love, encouragement, supportiveness, patience and the like. It does not matter what I *believe* I am like – I can *find out* for myself what I am like through meditation techniques, and the support of a suitable teacher. Nor does it matter as much what others believe I am like, when I am fully equipped to find out for myself. (Although I do need to listen honestly to others – see the section above)

As I watch myself I will have to be fair on myself and note the kindliness as well as the hostility. I have to be honest too, and note the hostility as well as the kindliness. Again, this is not about judgement and guilt or smugness. But, no cheating, as the tally mounts I get to know myself. At first, I don't have to do anything, just note. After a while, I may notice that I am beginning to catch myself out *just as* or even before the negative or positive action. (Later on, in Book 2, we shall develop this much further with technique of 'insight meditation'.) I may begin to get a feel for where I am on the axis, and I may begin to question whether I *have* to be at a particular location along it.

It is true that particular circumstances will have an impact on which pole I appear to be gravitating towards, but I may be drawn towards using that as an excuse. What we shall find is that I do not *have* to react, for example, in a hostile way, even under provocation. Here is a story from the Buddha's teachings to make this point graphically.

Classical Story: Refusing Anger

> Once the Buddha was abused by a brahmin [member of the priestly caste] who was angry that his relative had left home to become a follower:
> “When he had finished speaking, the Buddha said to him: ‘What do you think, Brahmin? Do your friends and colleagues, kinsmen and relatives, as well as guests come to visit you?’
> ‘Sometimes they come to visit, Master Gotama [Buddha].’
> ‘Do you then offer them some food or a meal or a snack?’
> ‘Sometimes I do, Master Gotama.’
> ‘But if they do not accept it from you, then to whom does the food belong?’
> ‘If they do not accept it from me, then the food still belongs to us.’
> ‘So too, brahmin, we – who do not abuse anyone, who do not scold anyone, who do not rail against anyone – refuse to accept from you the abuse and scolding and tirade you let loose at us. It still belongs to you, Brahmin!’” (SN, vol. 1, p 256).

Anger is one of a family of ill-feelings: pique, resentment, fury, grudge, vengefulness, irritation, frustration, grievance, bitterness, contempt, exasperation, hatred, lasting disappointment and so on. The Angry Family are in pain, and they share their pain everywhere. Then there is the Kindly Family: kindness, peacefulness, equanimity, joy in someone else’s happiness, love, appreciation, respect, cordiality, amiability, acceptance, forgiveness, patience and so on. The two families live in the same house.

The Angry Family are holding feelings against others, and not noticing that they thereby hold them against themselves.

Meanwhile, the Kindly Family first learned not to hold feelings against others, and then had to go deeper and learn not to hold them against themselves. Living as they do, in the same house, the Angry Family cannot really hurt the Kindly Family, because the latter does not accept the abuse, but remains peaceable and kind. The Angry Family gradually learns that it is only hurting itself and expressing its own pain, and finds that the Kindly Family, being what it is, is more than happy to help. This might be a story of the human race.

Intention

Anger, of course, is nearly always some form of frustration over not getting what one wants, or over getting landed with what one does not want. When my intentions (which I am clinging to) are thwarted, a beast rears up in me.

The Buddha's teaching wraps up a bundle of fundamental intentions quite neatly and comprehensively in what may be called 'The Eight Worldly Intentions'. These are in Table 4.

Table 4: The Eight Worldly Intentions

CLINGING	REJECTING
Pleasure	Pain, discomfort
Praise	Blame
Fame	Bad reputation, obscurity
Gain	Loss, want

We only have to look around us, at the activities of corporations, advertisers, salespeople, shopping, the media, the entertainments industry, crime – and look into ourselves, of course – to see these eight intentions energetically at work. This is not to moralise from on high. It is, as a matter of fact, what we find within.

We tend to hold before us the image of the perfectly happy human being as one who has 'got it all': who indulges pleasure regularly (tasty food, fun, sex, luxuries, etc.), who is praised by everyone for their success and achievements, who is a celebrity, world-renowned, receiving accolades from every quarter, and who gains wealth, possessions and physical attractiveness.

The miserable wretch, who apparently suffers a fate worse than death, is the one who is in discomfort and pain, blamed by everyone for their failures, who is either humiliated or living in complete obscurity, and who is poor and physically ugly.

This is the world wholly created by our human intentions. It is our chosen hell. We intend to escape from pain and discomfort by seeking pleasure, escape from blame by seeking praise, escape from obscurity by seeking fame and escape from want and loss by seeking wealth. When we have gratified our intentions we come up against the truth: we may not be any happier, we may feel the insecurity of losing what we have, and we may also become aware that nothing is permanent in any case.

So, in this frame of mind, we may be quite mystified by the fact that poor people often seem happy, and rich ones often unhappy, and that if the rich are sometimes happy it is not because of their wealth but despite it. We may wonder at how much the rich and comfortable have to spend on security systems, body guards and insurance policies. We may scratch our heads trying to remember the name of someone once famous, and shake our heads at how those who were once praised for their success are blamed for the failure that suddenly pulls them down.

But perhaps we should really wonder why it is that we wonder, when *we* set up the fantasy in the first place.

Authenticity

It seems then that we are quite genuine about our inauthenticity, quite sincere about our insincerity to the true nature of life. When the Buddha spoke of 'ignorance' he was not insulting us, but was speaking honestly and accurately of our state of mind and the behaviour that flows from it. He was once in that state himself. Six years of determinedly looking into himself by himself changed that state. (Of course, he also had the benefit of previous spiritual traditions and teachers.) It was not so much a change from one state to another as a letting go of everything that stood in the way of seeing the truth of human life, including his very identity. He had to be strongly self-aware, watching his own assumptions, attitudes and reactions, and acknowledging rather than rejecting them.

In short, the Buddha had to learn to be completely authentic, utterly sincere with himself. He learned that there were different methods of doing this, some more helpful than others, and then decided to share these ways with us. What it amounts to, as we shall see in Book 2, is calming and concentrating the mind, penetrating the movements of the mind, understanding their fleeting and insubstantial nature, and eventually seeing directly that none of these movements need be 'me' or 'mine'. At this critical point one may be ready for kind of gratitude that transcends mundane thankfulness (Book 3).

So, one might say, my behaviour operates at three levels of sincerity and insincerity. As a child I may be completely sincere, in the naïve way that is based on the assumption that the world is, or at least can be, as I would like it to be. Gradually, I learn that it is not and cannot be as I would like it to be. I have to accommodate to that fact. So, I split myself into two. I grow a public face: I am tensely polite, habitually pretend, act out a role that's not completely 'me', hide or deny my feelings, act out passive aggression when I am frustrated, conform, keep in the running, and generally try to be 'a nice person' in the eyes of others.

Arriving home from work, the mask slips, and my personal face emerges, I can 'be myself'. I am still in the middle level, in which being myself means following my mood, just being whatever grabs me at the time: kind, cruel, patient, impatient, gentle, angry, helpful, obstructive and so on. This unleashed moodiness is very much celebrated as good and natural in our society. This is not surprising since having to maintain a public face and a social role is stressful, and letting one's moods take over is such a relief - for a while. And, of course, it may not be such a relief for others in the immediate environment, such as one's family.

The Buddha's Unusual Way opens up a third, deeper level. At this level my public/personal split evaporates. I am neither my polite self nor my moody self. I neither have to maintain a false image nor let my jolly and grumpy moods run amok. Somehow I have found a refuge from which I can watch the entire tragicomedy. I sincerely and compassionately watch what my thoughts, feelings and sensations are up to, and get to know them and their primordial ways. Instead of escaping for a while from boredom by attaching to excitement, or escaping for a while from excitement (which I now call 'stress') by attaching to boredom (which I now call 'relaxation'), I learn release from the merry-go-round of clinging and rejecting.

If I am sick on the see-saw, there is a solution: I can get off it. I am not the see-saw itself.

Exercise: Mindful Action

I sit down alone and review the last week. I think of my encounters, tasks and demands one at a time. I try my best to think of *my* role in these, not the role of others. I ask myself how much in the last week I have taken from others, and how much have I given. Before starting I have to reassure myself that this is not about praise and blame, defending myself or congratulating myself. It is about honestly understanding myself, with no praise or blame attached. Giving includes a smile, encouragement, assistance, time and effort, and use of one's belongings. Taking includes snubbing someone, demeaning someone or their efforts, avoiding the giving of assistance, time and effort. Once I have made the 'tally' I do not have to do anything with it, or feel anything about it, just acknowledge it.

CHAPTER 5
HOW I WORK

Everything that we have considered about speaking and acting so far is just as true in the workplace and of work generally. Turning our attention to the work I do 'for a living' is to bring the social dimension of my identity into focus.

PROGRESS?

It may come as a surprise to discover that the Buddha's teachings embrace the question of livelihood or work. Of course, he lived in a society very different from our own. It was very rural with a large number of people involved in subsistence agriculture. However, his society was beginning to urbanise into towns, although there was nothing like the industries, cities, banks and corporations of today. He probably could not have even imagined the kinds of work many of us do today, and the sheer complexity of it would have baffled him.

Still, the Buddha was a spiritual teacher, not an economist or sociologist, and what he has to say about the fundamental human condition is as relevant today as in his time. So maybe he *could* have imagined the general trend, if not the details. The trend to self-destruction was clear to him. It follows from the logic of the grasping and craving human condition. He would recognise its humanity, even if he would not know what a 'Double Hamburger and French Fries' is, what an ATM is for, or how it is possible to speak to someone in another country by holding to one's ear a small shiny object bearing numbers 0 to 9. Clinging, rejecting and ignorance would, if anything, be even more 'in his face' today. Progress would just be more of the same, but much bigger. Could he conceive the intensity of hatred behind the Holocaust, or that of the greed behind Wall Street, or that of the ignorance behind the nuclear arms race and the impending climate catastrophe?

If he were here with us now and we were to ask whether he thinks that the human race is on the whole more enlightened, what do you think he would say? Cleverer certainly, but wiser? Smart technological wonders abound, but ignorantly we take technology to be the *purpose* of our civilisation rather than one *means* among others for attaining civilization.

One thing that might intrigue the Buddha is that human beings *choose* to earn their living working in Wall Street, to work at making nuclear weapons, and to work at persuading people to eat more processed flesh of cows and sheep. As he notes that a J. Robert Oppenheimer becomes a celebrity for designing a weapon for the mass destruction of innocents, that a Milton Friedman earns a world prize for celebrating Wall Street and the *non*-altruism of corporations, and Saatchi and Saatchi was acclaimed for their ability to persuade millions to act in favour of their cravings and fantasies (before it collapsed of its own greed), he might just give a knowing nod and mutter 'Well, I told you so'. And we might ask him, 'And what should we do, then?', to hear the reply 'Let's start again, yet again, shall we?'.

What would strike him more than anything perhaps, is not the concentration and collectivisation of human harms in social catastrophe so much as how the humdrum work of millions of human beings has become separated both from its source and sustenance and from its consequences. We are all sleepwalking in an increasingly fragile organisational complexity. And it cannot go on.

We find some clue to the Buddha's thoughts on the matter, but they are incommensurate with our contemporary predicament. It appears that he mentioned a number of kinds of livelihood which bring harm at once to the workers and to the recipients of the work: dealing in weapons, dealing in humans, dealing in living beings, and dealing in intoxicants and poisons. We certainly still recognise these in contemporary forms, greatly intensified: global arms trade, human trafficking, mass underpaid 'casual labour' and child labour, factory farms, alcohol, cigarettes, cocaine, sleeping pills, etc. He also mentions several dishonest means of gaining wealth: practising deceit, treachery, soothsaying (quackery), trickery, and usury (lending at an interest). Telling lies and doing harm by means of one's work is the kernel of his concern.

There are many in our society today who see nothing to concern ourselves with in any of these. Indeed, all of these are perhaps the mainstay of our 'national interest', 'economic development' and 'economic growth'. At the same time, we have to remember that the Buddha's practice does not entail moralising or condemnation. Like Socrates (who was a Greek contemporary of his), the Buddha maintains that all those activities that some of us call 'sin' or 'evil' are all plain ignorance. The 'worse' they appear to be, the deeper the ignorance they flow from, the greater the compassion we may feel for ourselves. Condemnation has not worked, but insight and compassion are worth a try.

WORKING WITH IGNORANCE

In what way is the work many of us do in the modern world based on 'ignorance'? Surely it is not ignorance to take the opportunities provided by our society to purchase food and shelter, accumulate some wealth and belongings, make ourselves more secure, and have some fun? Isn't the Buddha the one who is being unrealistic about life and work?

We have to go back to the 'three levels' mentioned in the last section. This 'three level' way of seeing things could be applied to almost any aspect of life, but here we are thinking of work in particular. We could label these three levels, the naïve, the manipulative and the insightful, but taking care not to run off with the various connotations of these words before even considering precisely what is being said *here*.

At the first level there is the naïve ignorance of taking the world of work for granted, accepting uncritically that there is a range of jobs 'out there' and I should choose one. Choose 'the best one for me' and 'success' will follow.

At the second level, comes the realisation 'with experience' that work is suffused with conflicts, unfairness and disappointments. Whereas before I was naïve, now apparently I am worldly-wise. I am learning to manipulate the situation to my own advantage, to 'survive'. While I look back, and think I am now less ignorant than before, in fact I have reacted against my previous state by adopting a stance *against* the world: a stance which floats somewhere in a brew of caution, disappointment, manipulativeness, pessimism, fear, cynicism, hardness and defensiveness. I take this to be knowledge or even 'wisdom' i.e. worldly-wisdom. This arises purely by a reactive contrast with what I now regard as the naïveté of childhood and youth. I could stay in this condition the rest of my life, and many do, and some gather more and more negativity as they look forward to 'retirement' and go into old age. But they need not. However, to go beyond this attitude to life I need to *see* it as a pattern of life-reactions. I need to rise above it. How do I do that?

At the third level, I deeply question the conception of what is 'best for me'. It might gradually dawn on me that if it is true that I, like all humans, have a strong inclination to clinging and rejecting then why should that inclination stop simply because I am at work? The same applies to everyone else at work. What happens to us all when all that clinging and rejecting is added up and collectivised in an 'organisation'?

Maybe the way out is in learning to let go both of trying to counteract every clinging with a rejection and every rejection with a new clinging; instead, standing aside and watching my reactions and attitude, at least now and then. From this viewpoint what previously looked like knowledge is now revealed as a deeper form of ignorance than the one I was immersed in as a child or youth. I may even congratulate myself with the thought 'As a child I was happy in my innocence, but now I know what the world is *really* like…' That is, I take myself to be knowledgeable but unhappy. But that's impossible. From the third level viewpoint true happiness and real knowledge turn out to be the same thing.

The second-level ignorance which permeates work these days is multiplied a thousandfold by complex organisation. Whereas once upon a time in my dullness of mind I could destroy *myself*, and perhaps a few others around me, now we can heap all our ignorance up in wondrously complicated and sophisticated ways and destroy the entire human race without realising it. This is called progress. It is a progress we neither intended nor created, but stumbled into by not paying attention. It is a spiritual and ethical regression.

So, to update the Buddha's list of harmful and inauthentic ways of going about a living we should all perhaps ask ourselves: What do I do for a living? Why do I do it? What is its purpose? What is the point of my employing organisation? What impact does it have on society, on other creatures, on the environment, on future generations? How is it connected with what others do? Are those connections harmful? Is harm only to be found in the direct actions of the arms trader and drug trafficker or also in the considered decisions of the suit-and-tie executive in his immaculate office who follows precisely the procedures, the law and the code of conduct of his profession?

The ethical issue of livelihood in this epoch is generally not about going out and doing a bad thing to make money, but not having any ethical idea at all about what my work is for, what it is doing to me (or making me) as a human being and its wider consequences for my fellow creatures. This is a precarious position for a global civilization to be in. Our problem is not the economy, it is not 'peak oil', it is not technology – *we* are the problem.

Increasingly we work in order to consume, and we consume in order to … well … in order to consume. Can we escape the powerful attraction of this black hole of our own making?

Exercise: Mindful Livelihood

> Next time we go to work let us try out some of these questions on ourselves. Why do I personally do the work that I do – what are my intentions? Am I, through the very nature of my work, manipulating others to my own ends? Am I being carried away with this just because everyone else is doing it, or am I reflecting on it? What is the ultimate purpose of the organisation I work for? Does it do harm to people, to their health, to their understanding, to other creatures and the environment? Is there something else I could do for a living that is less harmful in its indirect consequences? Am I stressed out by my work, and what is the rationale for that – is it worthwhile? Is it making me a calmer, a more insightful and compassionate human being? Is it contributing to peace for me, for the organisation, for society – and are these the same thing? If not, which is or ought to be the most important? Who takes responsibility for the consequences of my organisation's activity? Do I, at least in part? What will my work mean to my grandchildren and great-children, and all future generations?

The Buddha himself was an itinerant monk of sorts, and it will be said that he did not have a livelihood, so can hardly be an expert on the meaning of work. During his wanderings the Buddha once joined a workers' food-distribution line in order to receive a monk's alms. The brahmin responsible took issue with him. Here's the story.

Classical Story: How the Buddha Ploughs

[Brahmin:] 'Recluse, I plough and sow, and when I have ploughed and sown I eat. You too, ascetic, ought to plough and sow; then, when you have ploughed and sown, you will eat.'
[The Buddha replied:] 'I too, brahmin, plough and sow, and when I have ploughed and sown I eat.'
[Brahmin:] 'You claim to be a man who works the plough, but I do not see your ploughing. If you're a ploughman, answer me: How should we understand your ploughing?'
[The Buddha replied:] 'Commitment is the seed, austerity the rain, wisdom is my yoke and plough; the acknowledgment of ignorant action is the pole, mind the yoke-tie, mindfulness my ploughshare and goad.... Energy is my beast of burden, carrying me to security from bondage. It goes ahead without stopping to where, having gone, one does not sorrow.'
(SN vol. 1, pp 267-8, adapted by GH)

CHAPTER 6
EFFORT

EFFORT AND NON-EFFORT

Moving from darkness in an enlightening direction is also work. It is work on myself, and work for and with others. The Usual Way of work may often, on deeper reflection, be a kind of anti-work, a counter-productive effort, and energy spent on digging a hole that serves no purpose and is not filled up, until we fall into it.

'Energy is my beast of burden', says the Buddha. We all know that energy is our beast of burden, but is our beast carrying the burden even vaguely in the same direction as the Buddha's? Peace, insight and compassion are not possible without effort, and that is why the Buddha emphasized it as an essential part of the Unusual Way. A 'meditation' which is an occasional relaxation from stress, so that I can return refreshed to the very causes of the stress until the next break (or breakdown), is not what the Buddha was talking about. The Buddha was not teaching us how to take a rest on the merry-go-round but how to stand back from it. Deeper than that, he was showing us that there is no merry-go-round, except for the one we create by our constant craving.

It is not a case of giving up my work and becoming a monk or a nun. It is a matter of reappraising the meaning of the work I do as I continue to practise the Buddha's way. Whether as a result of this practice I do my work in a different spirit, or change it in some practical way, or even give it up entirely, is not for an 'enlightened person' to *tell* me to do. There is no value in that. The value is in discovering it for myself, even if I need a hand.

It is the same with effort generally. The effort that may be expended in doing what someone tells me is 'right', or even in doing what I tell myself is 'right', is not always going to be any less harmful than the same effort expended on doing what is 'wrong'. It may even sometimes be more harmful. History is littered with the damaging self-righteousness of accusations, correcting others, evangelism, just wars, inquisitions, bombing the innocent, crusades and guilt-ridden self-flagellation.

Thus, we have already seen that the effort required of self-liberating speech, action and livelihood is not so much the effort of doing but of *not-doing*. That is, the effort of letting go. This is not a 'Don't do this or that!', but a case of the 'this' and 'that' simply not arising in the first place. It is not so much a matter of having to hold my tongue in speaking ill of someone, but of it just not occurring to me to speak ill. The former is an attempt to counteract doing by rejecting the doing. The latter is neither a doing nor a rejecting of doing.

It is the same with meditation. The effort required is not that of the attaching, grasping, clinging, craving and rejecting that goes with building up, protecting and reassuring myself. The universal tragicomedy of human beings expending over the millennia just about enough energy to steam the Earth in its own atmosphere now perhaps gives us a vantage point to pose two questions: energy for what? And, what kind of energy is really worth expending? The latter follows from the former.

Once we question the effort of getting more and more, because of the bigger and bigger black hole it threatens us with, we then have to question what *kind* of energy is appropriate to civilized life. It cannot be the energy of grasping. Nor can it be the energy of rejecting. It must be quite different: it is surely the effort of not-grasping.

If you think that it requires no effort to learn to let grasping lie where it is, think again. Here is a parable.

Parable: The Floating Man

> Ade is teaching Wu to swim. Wu is very nervous, and fears drowning. Any time his face goes under water he panics and grasps at anything he can hold on to. Ade provides a kickboard and Wu holds on tightly to that. After some weeks, Wu does know that if he is going to swim then he has to let go of the kickboard. When he tries this however he panics and grabs hold of Ade's hair instead, holding her under water. Ade recovers and jokes that Wu really should not try to drown his teacher. 'Sorry, but I was scared! Oh, I'll never swim!', says Wu. 'That's the only problem you really have: fear', says Ade, 'Do you realise you can already swim, you just need to let go'.
>
> Ade explains that Wu is trying too hard, grasping at the water, grasping at doing the right leg and arm motions, grasping at the bottom or side of the pool, grasping at Ade's hair, as well as rejecting his own clumsiness and failure. She suggests that Wu lie back in the water with his head back, his body in a relaxed horizontal position, and very gently move his arms and legs together in one motion like a sleepy frog. Ade shows him, and this action of (almost) not-doing anything seems to work. This also requires an effort, but it is not the effort of 'overcoming' the water in order to make progress from A to B. It is instead, for Wu, the effort of trusting that the water will hold him, because he and the water are made that way. After all, they grew up together, you might say.

I need not cling to the water to force it to work for me, which is futile. I need not reject the water as stuff that threatens me with death by drowning. I need not even reject my futile grasping, for which I might instead feel compassion. What would benefit me is learning to let go of clinging *and* rejecting, so that this 'water

v. me' problem does not arise at all. I can already float; what 'problem'! This letting go requires an effort, and it is the kind of effort involved in meditation. (This special effort of trusting comes up again in Book 3.)

It would be really useful if we could devise a way of looking into effort, watching how it is from one moment to the next being harnessed for this, but not for that. That will take us deeper into the nature of meditation, attention and non-attention (Book 2). But first we need to take our making of effort to a deeper, more fundamental level.

Ethical Detox

Classical texts of the Buddha Dharma often speak of 'purification', a kind of ethical 'detox', as a prelude to meditation and other practices. Admittedly, in the West our culture is not in a mood to give this much serious consideration. Western culture is now fundamentally hedonistic i.e. it seems obvious to the vast majority that the main aim of life is fun. So 'obvious' is this that any alternative does not appear 'realistic'. For many it makes perfectly good sense to make truly heroic efforts in 'physical fitness', but it is patently silly to spend any effort at all on moral fitness. While there is nothing wrong with fun now and then it is hardly sustainable as the moral foundation of a person's life, let alone a civilization. The West is probably the first society in the history of the world dedicatedly to attempt this feat for the last half-century. So, effort is apparently well understood – it is what is involved, for example, in packing one's belongings into a confined space and hauling them across the planet at 500 miles per hour and back for something called 'a holiday', which is often so exhausting that one needs a good rest before returning to work.

Now, we just have to imagine taking, say, 10% of that energy, and using it to undertake some internal travel – a journey into oneself. Of course, just as that holiday far away often turns up unpleasant things like cockroaches, malaria, sunburn, diarrhoea, a noisy hotel and theft, so too the internal travel has its unexpected discomforts. The difference is that the 'holiday' is often motivated by the fantasy of advertising brochures (and perhaps a dose of rivalry with one's neighbours and colleagues – 'Oh, you went to Swanage … mmmh … we went to Bali'). Discomforts are definitely not in the brochure, and must be stamped out with complaints or defended against with insurance policies. The internal travel, however, is motivated by a call to get to grips with what this life really is. (Surely, it can't be holidays all the way down?)

To re-orientate oneself in life it is not sufficient to pay attention only to one's efforts 'out there in the world', such as the effort involved in studying for an exam, in a sport or in furthering one's career. One has to go deeper. The reason for this is that the outer efforts are working in concert with very powerful inner energies, of which we may be unaware. Inner energies patterns which continue year after year become so much a part of us that we may not see that *that* is where a lot of our total effort is going. In a way, who we are is defined by these inner energy fields, so it is really important to become aware of them and choose to re-direct them or let go of them, if we see this is necessary for peace and wisdom.

Habitual energy fields

Some of this habitual energy may be unhelpful or even self-destructive, and sometimes without your knowing it, or knowing it only dimly. Some of it may be helpful. The unhelpful and the helpful efforts may be at war with each other within yourself, and this is the basis of much dissatisfaction, frustration and anger directed at others. If under certain social circumstances this inner-conflict anger is collectivised and seized upon by power-hungry politicians it can be channelled and aimed at a scapegoat social group, perceived as different in some way.

Nothing, then, could be more important than coming to see for oneself what pattern of habitual energies is at work within oneself. Without this inner 'clearing out', meditation will be difficult and may not work at all. It is a widespread misconception that one can start on a rather 'heady' kind of meditation or 'practise mindfulness' *without* first looking into one's deep seated pattern of reactions and endeavouring some deep re-orientation.

A person who functions on a balance of distrust and ill-will towards others over loving-kindness towards others will not attain much enlightenment from practising meditation, even in one hundred years. A person who shifts that balance to loving-kindness will have benefited enormously, even if they never meditate.

So, what are these inner energies, and what can be done with them? In order to get clear about them some Dharma teachers distinguish between 'unwholesome' and 'wholesome' states. These words might have for some people a rather 'Mary Poppins' quaintness about them, like many other terms which our values-impoverished society feels almost embarrassed by: 'honour', 'noble-mindedness', 'tenderness', 'commitment', 'diligence', 'self-discipline' and the like. So that I don't ring the wrong bells, I choose another pair of words: unfruitful and fruitful. Some states do not give fruit to peacefulness, wisdom, compassion and spiritual understanding. Others do give fruit to these.

One can look at the flowers on an apple or plum tree and hope that fruit will one day appear there. The potential is there, but the fruit is not … not yet. One of three things can happen. A fine fruit will grow; no fruit will grow at all; a deformed or diseased fruit will partially grow before withering and possibly infecting the other fruit. What happens will depend on a number of interrelated conditions including, most importantly, how I take care of the fruit tree. First we deal with unfruitful states.

UNFRUITFUL STATES

If we think about the fruit tree about to bear fruit, there is another distinction which cuts across whether it is unfruitful or fruitful. Has the unfruitfulness or fruitfulness arisen yet? Is it just a potential, hidden from view in the bud or flower, or is it actual? Plums don't grow on apple trees, and apples don't grow on plum trees. If we have a plum tree in flower, we assume that plums will appear when the tree begins to fruit. It is often the same with good fruit and bad fruit. A particular tree may always produce small untasty fruit, whatever one does. When the tree has not yet borne fruit, that smallness and un-tastiness are not apparent, they have not arisen. We might say the smallness and un-tastiness are 'unarisen'.

This is how it is with us too, from a personal character point of view. In a sense, our 'goodness' is arisen or unarisen, and our 'harmfulness' is arisen or unarisen. The Buddha teaches us to examine all four and indicates how we should deal with them. He said:

> "And what, friends, is right effort? Here one awakens enthusiasm for the non-arising of unarisen harmful unwholesome states, and he makes effort, arouses energy, exerts his mind, and strives. He awakens enthusiasm for the abandoning of arisen harmful unwholesome states, and he makes effort, arouses energy, exerts his mind, and strives" (MN, p 1100).

To make things easier to grasp the Buddha mentioned five unfruitful states in particular, which are always hindrances to meditation and indeed to spiritual understanding. They are:

(1) desire
(2) ill-will
(3) dullness or laziness

(4) worry or anxiety
(5) doubt or indecision.

This is not that complicated, if we recall his simple teaching that craving is at the bottom of it all. What the five amount to perhaps is this: we want more of stuff, we get frustrated and angry when we don't get more (or can't get rid of what we don't want), we get tired out chasing around after what we want (or rejecting what we don't want), we worry about whether we can or will get what we want or about losing what we have, and finally we doubt that there is any other way of going about life. (This *is* the other way i.e. the practices in this Manual on the Buddha's teaching.)

Unarisen unfruitful states

So this is how it works: Every hindrance begins (for our purposes here) with a mere 'sign', a flicker of the senses – a sight, sound, touch, taste, smell, a sense-memory. (We may recall here what was said earlier about the torch light in the darkened room.) We might think of these flickers as little fly-papers to which the mind attaches, and in attaching thereby shuts off its natural openness.

When that which is a sign of one of the five hindrances to meditation first appears, then *before* the harmful state of mind arises the person sees the risk *in* the sign, and immediately lets it go, not letting it develop into associated ideas and feelings. In other words, the senses are guarded, but not in a tense or hostile manner. A sign which could lead to trouble is nipped in the bud, so it gets no chance to give rise to desire, greed, lust, anger, jealousy, apathy, anxiety, etc. After all, even with a kindly disposition, one does not let just *anything* through one's front door – a rabid dog, a stranger with a knife, or for that matter a smiling salesman.

If it is too late, and the grasping state has *already* arisen in one's mind, then more effort is required to dispel the associations which are growing around the original sign. There are a number of ways of doing that. As with an infected fruit on a tree, the longer one leaves it, the more it develops, the more the effort required to get rid of it. To make this clearer we need some examples. Here is an example of the hindrance of anxiety or worry.

Story: Nip it in the bud

> When under stress or unhappy, Joe occasionally finds himself becoming fixated on something very trivial. This most often happens when he has gone to bed and is about to sleep. On one occasion he remembered something that a senior colleague, Jan, had said at work earlier that day. He was not sure whether the colleague meant to blame him for an untoward event at work or not. He re-played it in his mind, trying to remember whether the tone was sarcastic, what the precise words used were, what the context was, what had previously been said by others, whether other colleagues generally thought he was negligent at work, and so on. He began to feel insecure and wondered what would be said about him at the annual review. He began developing a feeling of dislike towards Jan. 'Why can't Jan be clear? Is Jan saying other things behind my back!' In this agitated state Joe did not sleep for several hours.

This may seem like a silly story about a silly man. Unfortunately, millions of people suffer torment from such fixations. Far more than that, this story even does service as a brief history of the human race.

It is an illustration of a much more general point about the human inclination to attach, to stick, in ways which become obstructive to spiritual understanding. What can helpfully be said about Joe's state of mind in this context is not intended to be primarily psychotherapeutic i.e. in the professional sense, but rather how all human beings can remove or mollify the conditions of attachment, craving and clinging. Clearly, it raises issues about the inner environment of anxiety in which clinging arises, and whether one can let go of clinging (i.e. not cling) the moment it shows some sign of arising, as well as whether anything can be done once it has arisen.

Things might be quite different, or at least easier, if Joe acknowledges this tendency to latch on in this way. Let's consider the unarisen state. He's lying in bed, lights off, and there is some low-level 'wandering of the mind' going on, but Joe has learned about the stickiness of certain thoughts. He knows that when he is anxious or upset he may be laying the ground for a 'latching on' to a recent memory. So, he notes whether he feels that way, and observes it if it is there. Observing the anxiety itself (but not the thing he may be anxious about) it subsides. If the anxiety subsides then those troublesome 'signs' are less likely to arise. Then, if even for a 'millisecond' there is a 'sign' of a sticky thought, he lets it go, perhaps by practising a simple meditation exercise (Book 2) or by putting his mind onto a completely unrelated object, whether a play of light in the window or a pleasant memory in his mind.

One only has to look at advertising to see how well the desires and fears of human beings have been understood by those who, far from wishing to allay them, wish to inflame them to their own ends of gain and power. It is designed, in the first instance, to make *unarisen* states of mind arise. Then, it is designed to intensify arisen states. Hardly any advertising is designed merely to inform. As we all know, it is designed to multiply and deepen our desire (wants) and do so by playing into a quite small set of habitual energies: sexual desire, desire for food and drink, desire for security… in short pleasure, praise, fame and gain and avoidance of pain, blame, obscurity and loss.

Our next exercise turns the tables on the advertisers. We can look at their advertisements and deploy them to understand ourselves and transcend the manner in which advertisements endarken us. Thus the advertisement becomes a supra-advert, to coin a word. A use of the advertisement that is 'above or beyond' the advertisement itself, and a means by which we re-empower ourselves. Thus any advertisement can become a means of liberation rather than imprisonment, and to be welcomed as a free teacher, a supra-advert.

Exercise: The Supra-advert

> Next time you are either walking down a railway or underground platform look at the poster advertisements and instead of simply reacting to the half-naked body-beautiful or noting the particular product being advertised do two quite different things:
>
> 1) Note what the initial 'sign' is (flesh cleavage, gleaming car, silky chocolate, whatever) and note your own reaction to it. You can ask yourself: 'What was the very first thing that I noticed?', 'Did I linger on it?', 'Did I have to linger on it?', and 'What feelings and thoughts did it evoke in me?'
>
> 2) Ask yourself whether the poster fits into one of these eight categories in what it is evoking (or trying to evoke) in you: pleasure-fulfilment, pain-avoidance, praise-fulfilment, blame-avoidance, fame (popularity)-fulfilment, obscurity ('I'm a nobody')-avoidance, gain-fulfilment, loss-avoidance.
>
> For example, an insurance advert might carry a powerful image of loss-avoidance and/or pain-avoidance. An alcohol advert might carry one of pleasure-fulfilment and/or obscurity-avoidance. Note out of 10 or 20 posters which categories are most common. Maybe you will

notice some that don't fit into any of these categories, so you can create your own liberating supra-advert.

When you find you can do this, and it has thrown light on the way your own mind works, the next stage is to 'nip it in the bud', which means dropping the 'sign' the very moment it appears. You have to be quick. This is the effort of non-effort; so quick there is no real effort involved. Quicker than catching a ball thrown to you.

So, you walk through the tunnel onto Northern Line platform at Waterloo, your mind on the appointment you have to keep, and suddenly there is in your face a 3-metre high poster of a young half-naked woman (or man) with a seductive look and lying on a beach with a bottle of alcohol between her (his) legs. (If this does nothing for (to) you, good, but think of an advert that does arouse your interest, in order to learn about yourself.)

By now, with a little training, you have got used to this (if you weren't already). Instead of 'having a good look' or embarrassedly turning away, you did not even get as far as 'Whorrr! Look at that!' Instead in the time it takes to blink you have registered the initiating 'sign' of 'pleasure' and let it go. Not only your eyes, but your mind is elsewhere in a flash.

Sounds impossible? Well, just think that you already do it every day without noticing it, but not for the 'enticing' things but for the neutral or 'nasty' things. As we mentioned earlier, the senses dart quickly over all sorts of things and simply do not register them but immediately drop them because of the complete *absence* of any inclination of the mind to stick to them. Thus, it is hardly likely that walking down Oxford Street your vision would linger on a splatter of last night's vomit in the gutter and even less on a discarded piece of paper of no significance. While the vomit might be momentarily noticed and let go of, the piece of paper would almost certainly not be noticed at all.

So, just try it and keep trying it. You already know how to let go in milliseconds, it is your native effort of non-effort;

you just need to extend your application of this liberating technique. After all, what are advertisements but 'desire-me' psycho-tricks? Do we *have* to fall for them? And, it's not just about advertisements of course, but all of our daily experience. When you get to Book 2, you will see how important this control over attention is.

Some readers may object that this kind of exercise may make us quite neurotic, having the opposite effect to the one proposed, because I may become obsessed with trying to 'catch myself'. This is an understandable objection. However, one does not have to try and do this every waking moment of the day (unless, perhaps, one chooses a monastic life-style) but only sufficiently for the lesson to be learned. If I once had to make an effort to learn the 'times tables', and repeat '...6x7=42, 7x7=49, 8x7=56...' apparently without end, these days I hardly ever repeat any part of it, but nevertheless I do know my times tables for they have become part of my background knowledge and I have no neurosis about it.

Putting out of reach

It should be obvious that there is another simple (if not always convenient) method of not allowing unarisen unfruitful states to arise. It entails not putting oneself in a position where they will arise. Since we live in a consumerist society in which advertisers are continually giving us strong 'signs' this is not always easy. But we may become so immured in consumerist signals that it never occurs to us that there are lots of opportunities to shut them out or simply be where they are not.

A recovering alcoholic or cigarette-smoker knows that it is better not to be where the signs of these things are, or to avoid them, or to shut them out. For example, we can mute the TV when the advertisements come on. (On the other hand, we might look forward to the opportunity to practise the supra-advert technique!) We can avoid people and situations which 'drag us down', at least until we have the Dharma maturity to benefit from the lessons there might be in them.

There is a danger of being misunderstood here and in a number of ways.

Firstly, this is not just about advertising, but about all those signs and signals that we allow to give rise to thoughts and feelings which block our deeper understanding.

Secondly, I do know that many of us have become 'hardened' to advertising, and most people understand what advertisers are up to. However, research shows that advertising *does* on the whole have the effects that manufacturers and distributors want, and that is why they are willing to pay millions for advertising campaigns. Ask yourself how it is able to work, and whether it *must* work.

Thirdly, this is not at all about some kind of Victorian prudishness. You might say, 'What's wrong with being offered a bit of free sexual titillation on the underground platform? Or, some advice on insuring against a real risk such as a shark snacking on your buttocks while on holiday in Australia?' Well, nothing is wrong with it, except that when they all add up (especially for a child or young person) day after day and year after year, without awareness and challenge, one may find it harder and harder to find inner resources for some lasting meaningfulness in life.

The point of developing awareness of these unarisen and arisen states is that we would really like to be free, peaceful and wise; and all the money, food, sex, holidays, cars, insurance policies and cosmetic surgery in the world cannot achieve that except for the briefest of interludes.

Arisen unfruitful states

Let's say it's too late, and the associated thoughts and feelings have already started to arise. There are fine lines between unarisen, just arising and arisen. If you are already into the reaction 'Uh! Look at that!', then you are hooked. There are five techniques we can use for the unfruitful states which have arisen.

(1) Divert attention
(2) Use the opposite feeling to dispel the harmful feeling
(3) 'Stare it down'
(4) Marshal the forces of revulsion and dread
(5) As a last resort, suppress it (release it elsewhere non-harmfully).

All of these require effort on an ascending scale. The 'nip it in the bud' effort is tiny (or no-effort) by comparison. And all of them require that you first acknowledge that the state has arisen and may grow. (Some states, untreated and fuelled by other factors, may grow to horrendous proportions in which horrendous things are done, but let us consider the more ordinary situations, since this is not *primarily* a Manual on how not to murder a complete stranger on a bus or how not to bomb a country.) The ability to acknowledge comes earlier and earlier with practice, until one day one reaches the 'nip it in the bud' ability. The meditation practices considered in Book 2 will enable us to develop our abilities of attention, and this will help enormously with the matter of acknowledgement one's inner experience.

Diverting attention involves moving the attention as soon as possible on to something unrelated. It could mean moving it to something completely and utterly banal and paying close attention to it. You may find yourself investigating the delicate motions of a tiny and insignificant scrap of paper as a train approaches, or last night's vomit which has formed a fascinating stalactite on the edge of the platform. The latter is really an example of the fourth tactic, of marshalling forces of revulsion.

Have you ever thought that one way to put yourself off sexual thoughts when not-so-appropriately attracted to someone is to think of the 8-metre tube of foul-smelling matter just an inch or so under their clothes. Yes, there really is a very long smelly tube there… unless they are some kind of space alien. Still, one would not wish to dwell on this. It is just a passing supra-advert tactic. Or is it? For a fun-loving society the very idea of deliberately marshalling forces of revulsion is itself revolting, and enough to put one off 'Buddhism' for life. This tells us a lot about how *real* we have succeeded in making our fantasy lives.

Using the opposite feeling to dispel the harmful feeling is worth a try with irritation, anger, envy, jealous and the like. Staring it down is not advisable with desire, but may work with other members of the hindering family of five, such as apathy and doubt. As a last resort, especially if thoughts of murder on the bus are getting a grip on you, suppress them and let the energy out harmlessly. However, hammering nails into an effigy in your back yard is only a stop-gap, and anyway you should be able to find other things to do with your time that are more conducive to enlightenment.

Making recommendations for dealing with arisen unfruitful states of mind does perhaps present life as a kind of obstacle course. However, if you allow it, it will be an obstacle course anyway, and the point is to find out and put into practice a way of not allowing it. Your life need not be all obstacle course, and so far as it is one you can just *watch your experience* of the obstacles and ask yourself where they are actually located at any particular moment.

Exercise: Tactics for the obstacle course

Try the above five techniques in the following situations.
(a) Getting out of bed when you really don't want to: try the 'ignoring of sign' or 'nipping in the bud' i.e. just get up before a thought or feeling arises. You have to be

quick. The moment the thought arises 'Oh no! I have to get up!' is the moment that the suffering starts.
(b) Seeing/smelling food which you really don't need: try engendering the opposite feeling, such as an image of your giving it away to someone starving.
(c) Despising or looking down on someone: try feeling the opposite, some kindliness and compassion, which is best done by *doing* something considerate for that person.

FRUITFUL STATES

Having dealt with some habit-energies which hinder meditation, we now turn to those habit-energies which are conducive to meditation and to the preparation for it. The Buddha put it in a nutshell:

> 'And what, friends, is right effort? .... He awakens enthusiasm for the arising of unarisen wholesome states, and he makes effort, arouses energy, exerts his mind, and strives. He awakens enthusiasm for the continuance, non-disappearance, strengthening, increase, and fulfilment by development of arisen wholesome states, and he makes effort, arouses energy, exerts his mind, and strives. This is called right effort' (MN p 1100).

First we shall consider the conducive states which have not arisen in us. In view of what we have just learned it should be plain that one reason that they do not arise, or not as often as we might expect, is that they are drowned out by the arising unfruitful states. So we have to harness in a unified effort these 'Four Endeavours' (to use the classical term for channelling unarisen/arisen unfruitful/fruitful states). If we can make even a little headway with this we shall find our meditation, when we get to it, is so much more beneficial.

Unarisen fruitful states

To arouse unarisen wholesomeness, we have to make room for them and invite them in. It is like planting seed in a seed box on the window sill. We can sit there and watch and watch, and we know the seeds are there. But how do we get them to show themselves? After all, it is not the seeds we want, but the flowers and the delicious fruit that emerge from the flowers as they wither away. Wishful thinking is not going to do it.

In the case of seeds certain factors have to be present, such as fertile soil, water, light and warmth and removal of competing shoots. And we have to go on nurturing and caring for the seedling, transfer them to a garden, care for the growing tree, the flowers and the fruit through the whole cycle of life. In the case of the seeds from which fruitful states of mind arise we need certain 'factors of enlightenment'.

The Buddha suggests that these factors are seven in number: mindfulness, the investigation of phenomena (mental analysis), energy, joyfulness, tranquillity, concentration and equanimity (balance, poise). This may sound like a tall order, but then ask yourself whether growing a Cherry tree is a tall order. Yes, and no, depending on how committed you are and how you go about it. Anyway, the classical 'seven factors' express matters in a rather an abstract way (and I explain them fully in Book 2). Let's simplify them by taking further the seed box image.

Parable: The Cherry Tree

> Imagine the whole life of a Cherry Tree. The bright flowers are those states of mind which give rise to the sweet fruit of spiritual understanding (see Book 3). The flowers are, then, the mindfulness and concentration
>
> (see Book 2) which precede such understanding. Joyfulness is the radiant colour of the flowers.

> Tranquillity is the peaceful refuge the tree provides for tired and hungry creatures. Equanimity is the balanced proportions of the whole flowering tree. 'Investigation' is the close attention the gardener has to pay (and indeed, you might say, that the tree itself has to pay) to the soil, buds, leaves and so on to ensure healthy growth. Energy is the power the tree has - nourished by water, nutrients and light - to grow and bear fruit.

We can now appreciate perhaps that nurturing unarisen fruitful states of mind is nine-tenths of the Buddha's instruction, and of this Manual too, I hope, as it attempts to capture and clarify his teaching for the current age. And we must assume that human beings everywhere at all times have the sort of latency to produce fruit in the same kind of (metaphorical) way we assume wild Cherry trees do. While farmers know in an abstract way that not every seed they wish to plant will grow, they can never know which ones for sure. So their actual practice is the generous and hopeful one that all are given that chance, for it is not in the farmer's gift to cause growth itself but only assist its conditions.

Unarisen fruitful states are assisted by letting go of the dominating role that desires have in life, letting go of ill-will and resentment, of apathy, anxiety and (gradually perhaps) letting go of the doubt that there is an Unusual Way that has nothing whatsoever to do with desires.

As in all the Buddha's teachings there is a 'roll-up your sleeves and do it' suggestion for sparking off unarisen fruitful states. It has been used world-wide by hundreds of generations of followers of his way, and is essentially no different from the exhortation by Jesus to love your neighbour as yourself. We may call it the practice of 'the cultivation of loving-kindness'. Here it is, significantly adapted, in the form of an exercise, which has several steps.

Exercise: Cultivating Loving-Kindness

Sit by yourself, or in a community of meditators, and close your eyes.

(1) Self: Imagine you are looking at yourself, encapsulating your whole life. Then take a deep breath in and let it out slowly, like a sigh. Then sincerely express good will to yourself in these inner words: 'Though I suffer from ignorance, may I *now* be peaceful, may I be happy, may I be free'. When you say it, mean it, and emphasize the word 'now'. Hold this for a few minutes.

(2) Disliked: Imagine you are looking at someone you do not (did not) get on with very well or not at all. Some feelings of discomfort or hurt may be involved. Then take a deep breath in and let it out slowly, like a sigh. Then sincerely say these inner words to that person: 'Though you suffer from ignorance, like me and all of us, may you *now* be peaceful, may you be happy, may you be free'. When you say it, mean it, and emphasize the word 'now'.

(3) Neutral: Imagine you are looking at someone you know only in passing, but perhaps see quite often, and that you have no like/dislike feelings about (the postman, perhaps). Then take a deep breath in and let it out slowly, like a sigh. Then sincerely say these inner words to that person: 'Though you suffer from ignorance, like all of us, may you *now* be peaceful, may you be happy, may you be free'. When you say it, mean it, and emphasize the word 'now'.

(4) Local View: Imagine you are in the air looking down on your local neighbourhood or town. Then take a deep breath in and let it out slowly, like a sigh. Then sincerely say these inner words to that neighbourhood: 'Though you suffer from ignorance, like all of us, may you *now* be peaceful, may you be happy, may you be free'. When you say it, mean it, and emphasize the word 'now'.

(5) Global View: Imagine you are on the moon looking at the whole planet earth, as in the famous photos taken by astronauts. Then take a deep breath in and let it out slowly, like a sigh. Then sincerely say these inner words to all the billions of human beings and creatures: 'Though you suffer from ignorance, like all of us, may you *now* be peaceful, may you be happy, may you be free'. When you say it, mean it, and emphasize the word 'now'.

It won't always seem appropriate to do such an exercise. Still, if you feel some persistent antipathy to this exercise, it might be worth asking yourself: 'Am I in an arisen unfruitful state?'

You may have to run through the description of this exercise a few times before you can do it without looking at the words as you carry out the exercise. The precise words don't matter that much, of course. What is essential is that you are making a genuine effort to expand feelings of good will outward from yourself to the whole human race, step by step. It is probably best done in a group of meditators with a facilitator taking everyone through the stages. It is important not to hurry, so that the whole exercise takes about 20 to 30 minutes.

Arisen Fruitful states

Once fruitful states of mind have arisen in you, such as a higher degree of kindliness, equanimity and so on (and correspondingly less distractedness, irritability, anxiety, etc.) then they should be sustained by continuing practice. That is, not just maintainable for a while, but *sustainable*. I quite like the way the Buddha expressed it:

> '..suppose a cloth were defiled and stained, and a dyer dipped it in some dye or other, whether blue or yellow or red or pink; it would look poorly dyed and impure in colour. Why is that? Because of the impurity of the cloth. So too, when the mind is defiled, an unhappy destination may be expected …[but].. suppose a cloth were pure and bright, and a dyer dipped it in some dye or other, whether blue or yellow or red or pink; it would look well-dyed and pure in colour. Why is that? Because of the purity of the cloth. So too, when the mind is undefiled, a happy destination may be expected' (MN, p 118).

So, one has to put the fruitful states on such a footing that they are not easily lost, dissolved or obliterated. Persistent but gentle effort (largely non-effort, letting go) can strengthen them, link them, bind them into a whole change of outlook, which is further reinforced by meditation (Book 2) and further spiritual practices and understanding (Book 3). Sustainability will depend on regularity of practice, practising with a community of like-minded people, and using what one has learned to facilitate the learning of the way by others, and dealing productively with setbacks in life. If one feels a waning of fruitful states, perhaps due to some stumbling-block in life, *that* in fact is the time to learn from the inner dimension of the outer turmoil, and make a special effort. After all, anyone would make a special effort if their own child were in danger of being lost.

Fruitful states can and should also be helped to arise and be sustained on the level of friendships, family, the workplace, civil groups, voluntary groups, artistic creativity, one's neighbourhood and the whole human race and environmental life. Things do not have to get busier and busier, greedier and greedier.

We can eat slowly and together, slow down our cities, slow down our travel, get to know our neighbours and neighbourhood and volunteer to assist those who are in the unhappy condition that we might be in ourselves later or at any time.

CONCLUSION: Last words before Book 2

To conclude, I shall try to summarise in two paragraphs all the teaching in Book 1 of this Manual, and then briefly lead it into Book 2.

To have spiritual understanding is to drop all divisions and boundaries and in so doing loss one's small grasping self, have compassion for all things, live in peace and lose one's dissatisfaction and fear of death. This is not a theory but a kind of holistic experience and outlook which a person can work towards. The work involved has been experienced and clarified by many spiritual teachers and taught by them in diverse manners. One such teacher, who gives us a great lead, is the man now known as the Buddha i.e. 'the awakened one'.

The Buddha's approach in helping others follow this life-work programme is to set it out in three dimensions: ethical, meditational and a special kind of holistic (non-dual) understanding. In the first book of this Manual we clarify the ethical dimension. This involves paying *deep attention* to what we say, how we act, what we do for a living, and how we deal with inner obstacles to spiritual understanding and, instead, develop its catalysts.

In paying this attention we learn how so much of our abiding dissatisfaction has its roots in ourselves, not outside. In particular, we are attaching, craving and clinging creatures in a reality which cannot be attached to, cannot be craved for and cannot be clung to.

We learn that an infinitely greater security and satisfaction lies not in holding on to the world, but living and working with it. In order to reach this deeply human outlook we have to work, not on the world 'out there', but on ourselves.

Only when we have learned about ourselves can work on the world 'out there' take a shape which truly fits our fundamental needs and our potential for love, because only then will it be based on the recognition of our inexplicably *human* limitedness.

The matters we have covered in this Book 1 are indispensable to the life-long path of enlightening yourself. You cannot do without them if you choose to embark on that path, but it is far from being enough. There is little point in thinking 'Well, I have read Book 1, got the picture, now on to Book 2' unless you have spent some time, at least some months, going through the book (or another one like it) and doing the exercises for significant periods of time.

Besides having some intellectual grasp, which can be lost in even a few days (as anyone cramming for an exam knows), the lessons have to sink into one's heart and muscle. If one reaches a point at which one can honestly say, 'Yes, I look at life rather differently now', then that may be the time to move on to Book 2.

Several times in this book we have seen how important it is to be able to do these:

1) Turn the mind inwards, on itself, as it were
2) Pay close and continuing attention to one's own inner awareness of thoughts, memories, feelings, sensations and so on.
3) Let go of attachment, clinging, craving and rejection
4) Concentrate and calm the mind
5) Question matters about oneself that one normally never questions.

Can these be clarified, made simpler, put together and presented in a way that enables all of us to *do* them, and do them together? Yes, they are called meditation, which comprises most importantly mindfulness and concentration. These are covered in Book 2.

Readers who have encountered discussions of 'impermanence', 'rebirth', 'emptiness', 'non-self', 'dependent origination' and so on, and have not yet found them in this book, will find them clarified in Books 2 and 3.

In this first book I may have given the impression that following this path is a serial manoeuvre: finish one before you start on the next. Now it is time to add a caveat to this. You will find that, for example, dealing with arisen unfruitful states (like irritation, or its big brother, anger) is not that easy, however hard you try. Well, there's good news. It gets easier as you follow the other steps (factors) of the way, so that the mindfulness and concentration involved in meditation play a powerful role in making the effort of 'ethical detox' lighter and more effective.

So the Unusual Way is not a ladder to Heaven, but an enlightening spiral of eternal return.

This completes Book 1 of a three-book series:

New Buddha Way
Book 1: Ethical Living

New Buddha Way
Book 2: Letting Go

New Buddha Way
Book 3: Letting In

ABOUT NEW BUDDHA WAY

For more information on New Buddha Way (NBW) and its activities see the website at: www.newbuddhaway.org or write to:

NBW
PO Box 125
West Molesey
Surrey
KT8 1YE
United Kingdom

ABOUT LALESTON PRESS

For other short and clearly written books on the Buddha's practice and its implications, and on related topics in ethics, culture and philosophy see the website of Laleston Press at www.lalestonpress.com or write to the above address.